James Vick

Practical Garden Points

James Vick

Practical Garden Points

ISBN/EAN: 9783337083366

Printed in Europe, USA, Canada, Australia, Japan

Cover: Foto ©Lupo / pixelio.de

More available books at **www.hansebooks.com**

Practical Garden Points

―――― BY ――――

PRACTICAL PEOPLE.

A COLLECTION OF PAPERS BY PRACTICAL GARDENERS
AND FRUIT GROWERS.

ILLUSTRATED WITH NUMEROUS ENGRAVINGS.

PUBLISHED BY
JAMES VICK SEEDSMAN,
ROCHESTER, N. Y.

CONTENTS.

VILLAGE IMPROVEMENTS, D, H. Roberts, M. D.,	1
VILLAGE IMPROVEMENTS, F. H. Hastings,	5
THE GLOXINIA, Elizabeth Luney,	8
THE CINERARIA, Charles E. Parnell,	13
ANNUALS IN THE WINTER WINDOW-GARDEN, Julia A. Beers,	16
WINTER SUPPLY OF VIOLETS AND PANSIES, Charles Everding,	24
CHRYSANTHEMUMS, L. Oakey,	29
THE CALCEOLARIA, Charles E. Parnell,	33
THE CYCLAMEN, Charles E. Parnell,	36
THE ROSE AS A HOUSE PLANT, Flora F. Dorwin,	39
THE ROSE AS A HOUSE PLANT, Charles E. Parnell,	44
THE STRAWBERRY, John F. Dayton,	47
THE RASPBERRY FOR MARKET, S. S. Crissey,	53
THE BLACKBERRY, N. B. Hollister,	57
APPLES, J. W. Lang,	63
GRAPE VINES, S. S. Crissey,	67
MUSHROOM GROWING, B. Fletcher,	70
GROWING MUSHROOMS, William Falconer,	73
ASPARAGUS, W. C. Steele,	77
PEAS, B. Fletcher,	82
ONION CULTURE, W. Abell,	84
FIELD CULTURE OF ONIONS, P. Carry,	86
CULTIVATION OF ONIONS, Charles E. Parnell,	88
RAISING ONIONS, A. Waldron,	92
CABBAGE, W. H. Waddington,	94
CELERY, Mrs. C. H. Root,	98
KEEPING CELERY IN WINTER, Richard Gamble,	101
ROOT CROPS, Robert J. Fleming,	103

INTRODUCTION.

The articles here collected and republished are, for the most part, Prize Essays, which first appeared in the numbers of VICK'S MAGAZINE. They have all been written by practical and experienced garden workers, and all the statements have been verified and will stand whatever tests may be given them. Knowing them to be intrinsically valuable, and that they offer much information in garden work that is not easily accessible, it is believed that good service has been done in thus presenting them again to the public in this form.

A few of the papers are not Prize Essays, but, as they show different phases of experience, they are valuable on that account.

The flowering plants to which special articles are devoted are, for the most part, those which, to the beginner, usually present some difficulties, and here the manner of overcoming them is distinctly pointed out.

In the same manner the instructions relating to vegetables are those most needful to the inexperienced. It is thought that this little manual will prove an acceptable and trustful companion to the young gardener and fruit grower, and as such it is sent on its way.

GARDEN ESSAYS.

VILLAGE IMPROVEMENTS.

What agencies and methods can the residents of villages employ to secure the practical effects of the most advanced ideas of sanitation and the proper horticultural embellishment of streets and grounds?

When families live remote from each other, as farmers do, they may be more independent, but when they congregate in villages there should always be municipal government with powers, among other things, to promote the beautiful, and to remove everything calculated to injure the health of the people. For municipal officers, good and wise men should be selected independently of party lines.

On private lots the largest liberty, consistent with the health and happiness of others, should be allowed. But the streets, alleys, public buildings and general healthfulness of the place should be delegated to the village authorities.

The most advanced ideas of sanitation require good drainage throughout every part of the village, not only of surface water, but also of all stagnant water beneath and near the surface. They also require pure water for drinking and culinary purposes. They require freedom from the offensive odors and noxious gases that arise from putrid decaying animal and vegetable substances. They require dry and well ventilated cellars. They require that the streets and grounds should have proper proportions of sunshine and shade.

Proper drainage is most thoroughly secured by cutting down the streets from eighteen inches to three feet or more. As the soil is plowed or loosened, those owning low lots will be glad to carry it away for filling and bringing such lots to a level with others.

Thus, the public expense becomes small, and the owners of lots are accommodated. The streets should be left higher in the center, and the water carried off along the borders next the sidewalk. The sidewalk should also be cut down, but not lower than the central part of the street. The grade should be sufficient to secure rapid and perfect drainage.

Dwelling houses should be built upon stone foundations and

stand high enough that the cellar may be drained, if necessary, into the street. The alleys running back of the lots should also be cut down, but not more than half as low as the street, and so graded as to drain freely to the street. All this drainage should have ample and free outlet beyond the village limits. Most villages are naturally so situated as to admit of this thorough surface or open drainage, and those not so should have a proper outlet secured, even at much expense. Farmers and gardeners near the village should be encouraged to drain all their low or level grounds with tile, as unhealthy effluvia or miasma may be borne in the air to considerable distances before losing its virus.

Last fall, I visited a small village in Indiana, where I had resided some fifteen years before. Meeting, upon the street, two physicians, old residents, I inquired how they were getting on. "Ah," said one of them, "the tile business has ruined this place for doctors. The farmers have found that good underground drainage ensures so much better and more certain crops that they have fairly riddled the country with tile, and the result is, we have not one case of ague or miasmatic fever now where we had twenty when you lived here." The other physician said he could testify that the statement was entirely correct and not overdrawn. This corresponds with the testimony of many others, and speaks volumes for the sanitary advantages of underdraining.

To secure good, pure water for drinking and culinary purposes, cities may have expensive waterworks, but villages of from five hundred to ten thousand inhabitants can seldom afford so great expense; they must rely upon wells, usually from twelve to fifty feet deep. That the water in these wells may be kept pure and sweet it is evident that no filth or organic matter should be allowed to enter and contaminate it. Liquids that filter through the soil soon become purified, but where an opening is made so that a stream passes, but little purification can take place. The roots of trees seeking moisture often find the well several rods distant, and in another direction the privy vault. When these roots decay a direct communication is made between them. Worms and insects, also, frequently fill the soil with pores. A stratum of sand or gravel may, and often does, connect wells and cess-pools all over the village. Pure water in the village wells requires that no privy vault be allowed below the surface of the ground. The importance of this point is so great that laws should be made and enforced prohibiting the sinking of any such vault. Privies should be placed upon the alleys, and so arranged that ashes or dry earth may be frequently thrown in to deodorize and disinfect them, and that the contents may be frequently and regularly carried beyond the village limits.

That these ends may be attained with as little expense as possible, all privies should be furnished with boxes or chests of the same size and pattern, easily removed to a wagon or dray in the alley. They should also be so planned as to give room for, and be furnished with a chest of dry earth, which should be kept filled. The seat should have hinges at the back that it may be opened up for the frequent introduction of dry earth.

The village authorities should see that the full chests are regularly carried away and empty ones put in their places, and also that the dry earth chests are replenished. Waste and slops from the kitchen and manure from the stable, should be placed handy to the alley, frequently mixed with lime, ashes or earth, and regularly carried away by the village authorities.

Now, all this may appear, at first thought, to be attended with considerable expense; but a manure manufactory beyond the village limits, where all this waste is stored and protected from the weather, would doubtless soon yield profits far exceeding all expense. After being once introduced and its workings understood, business men would probably be found anxious to obtain the privilege of removing all filth from the village for the profitable manufacture of fertilizers.

When the streets are graded, a space should be left along the sidewalk and next the street for the planting of trees. This should have plenty of good surface earth sufficiently enriched for the rapid growth of trees. The trees should be planted by the village authorities in straight rows, leaving ample room for sidewalks of good width, and they should be attended by the authorities afterwards. All planting, replanting and pruning should be done with an eye to symmetry and proper admixture of sunshine and shade. Citizens should be careful in planting trees and ornamenting their grounds not to introduce too much shade; plenty of sunshine being absolutely necessary to good health. For the streets, hardwood trees will be found the best. Sugar Maple and Norway Maple are excellent for all northern climates.

Parks in small villages should be situated for convenience, or, if possible, to command beautiful or grand scenery, and be made pleasant and attractive as places of resort. No cemetery should be allowed within three miles of the village. Streams of water passing through or near the village should be kept pure and sweet. No slaughter house should be permitted to be so situated as possibly to contaminate the water. Dead animals should be far removed from streams of water for burial. Beer and liquor saloons should be prohibited.

All public or private school houses, halls, churches or other places for congregation should be inspected by the authorities, who should require provision for ample ventilation.

By common consent business places and public or private entertainments should be closed at or before ten o'clock in the evening; this is important. The health of our young people especially requires that they should have plenty of good sound sleep, and in our villages the majority of the community consists of laborers, mechanics, or persons in business, that require early rising. A few successive nights of excitement and loss of sleep often lay the foundation for nervous diseases and general ill health.

Now, all these things are believed to be absolutely necessary to secure the practical effects of the most advanced ideas of sanitation; and, moreover, they are eminently practical. In the course of a few years the little extra expense would surely be repaid both in health and wealth. The clean, healthful, beautiful village would attract the best classes of citizens and promote its prosperity more than much larger sums frequently spent in other directions.

VILLAGE IMPROVEMENTS.

This question is one of great importance, and of increasing interest, as there is, at the present time, so much attention given to the improvement of villages and homesteads with their surroundings. The number of persons, happily increasing from year to year, who have a desire and a determination to make their homes pleasant and attractive, thus setting a good example to others, so far as their influence goes, are entitled to commendation and assistance, and help from suggestions of others. But in order to accomplish much in this way in a rural community, it would seem necessary to have a club or the concerted action of a few individuals, at least, who have a real desire to improve their town or village, making it attractive as a place of residence.

As an illustration of what may be accomplished by such an organization composed of a few intelligent and public spirited persons, whose efforts, and their results, have come under my own observation, an account is here submitted, hoping their success may stimulate others to do likewise.

At the time when the "Rural Art Club" was formed, some years ago, there was nothing about the village in the way of ornamentation very noticeable; one or two individuals, as in most villages at the time, had their front yards and perhaps small gardens, with the meager supply of shrubs and flowers to be obtained at that period. The green, or common, around which a greater part of the village was built, was correctly called the "commons," as it was free to travel in all directions, and cattle and pigs were by no means excluded from its use.

This common had been made into a beautiful park with a fine variety of trees and shrubs, with its walks and fountain, adding wonderfully to the appearance of the village and to the pleasure of the inhabitants, who feel a laudable pride in their park. The various streets leading to the village, and the new streets opened as the growth of the place required, have not been neglected, but embellished with suitable shade trees, and many of the beautiful homes on these streets bear witness to the taste and enterprise of the residents.

At the stated meetings of the "Rural Art Club," one, or more, essays by some of its members were read and discussed and any topic of general interest was published occasionally in the village paper, that those not members of the club might derive benefit from the suggestions presented.

As the old cemetery became crowded, and was itself a barren, unattractive spot, a rough, hilly tract of land of several acres, near the village, was secured, and an association formed, who laid it out and improved it for a new cemetery, making it a very pleasant and desirable place for its purpose, and one in which all feel a pride and interest.

As one improvement naturally leads to another, so, recently a system of water works has been furnished the inhabitants, adding to the health and convenience of all concerned.

Allowing that much may be done by individual effort towards beautifying and improving towns and neighborhoods, yet the combined labors of a few active and intelligent persons, who have the good of the public at heart, seem desirable and necessary in order to make rapid and permanent improvements in any village, both in the way of sanitation and making homes beautiful. Even a few persons who are willing to give a portion of their time and are generous enough to distribute to others such trees, shrubs and plants as they could easily spare, would contribute in no slight degree to the happiness of others, and be amply rewarded in the improved appearance of their neighborhood.

Of course, various methods will suggest themselves to such an association in order to awaken an interest in the public generally in all subjects pertaining to sanitation or rural art, such as occasional lectures by physicians of the place upon the general principles of drainage, location of wells and subjects relating to the health of families, with essays upon improving and decorating homes, illustrating and impressing upon all what may be accomplished by the judicious use of trees, shrubs and plants in rendering their homes pleasing and attractive. A few years of such persevering and systematic effort will result in wonderful improvement of neighborhoods, and prove a great means of education to the young.

Our laws at present in regard to cattle running at large, are such that the old, unsightly fence around every door-yard, is rendered unnecessary, and it is gratifying to see that they are gradually being removed, adding greatly to the beauty of a street. Every school district should take interest enough in the welfare of the children to plant trees about the schoolhouse, making it more comfortable and pleasant in every way.

Thus, briefly are presented the methods which, by experience, have been proved to be effective and expeditious in accomplishing many and important village improvements.

THE GLOXINIA.

Notwithstanding the fact that the Gloxinia is assigned a place among the stove plants in sundry catalogues, and is, undoubtedly a native of a very hot climate, it is one of the most satisfactory flowers known for window as well as greenhouse culture, requiring comparatively little care and attention in return for its brilliant blossoms and scarcely less beautiful foliage. The great variety of form and color exhibited in its flowers entirely precludes the idea of sameness, and gives to the cultivator the pleasure of ever looking forward to the development of new beauties in the growing plants. Of course, new varieties usually originate in seedlings, as the Gloxinia is not like the Petunia and many other flowers, inclined to sport. Any desirable kind can be propagated from leaf-cuttings, which strike readily, and will produce flowering bulbs for the following season.

The materials requisite for the growing of the Gloxinia from seed are really very few. First on the list is good seed, and I much prefer that ripened in summer or autumn for sowing the ensuing spring to that which is of greater age, as I do not think, judging from experience, that Gloxinia seeds retain their vitality so long as many other kinds. Secondly, a quantity of pure leaf-mold, as I

THE GLOXINIA.

confess to the heresy of not even requiring the prescribed leaven of sand for the growing of this plant to the size required for pricking out into pots. If, however, the leaf-mold cannot be obtained, then add a "dash of sand" to the mellow earth which must be used as a substitute. I like the leaf-mold better than any compost, no matter how nicely prepared, for, in the first place, when once saturated with water it retains the moisture for a long time, thus rendering unnecessary the frequent waterings so dangerous to tiny germinating seed, and, in addition to this, the leaf-mold, while so fine and soft that the smallest rootlet can easily push its way through it, is not porous, so that there is little danger of its swallowing the minute seed into fatal depths. Next in order comes the receptacle for the mold or earth in which the seeds are to be sown. For this purpose use a shallow box, not over three inches in depth, a cigar box, the bottom of which has been perforated with an awl or small gimlet, in order to admit water freely, will answer admirably and can be easily procured. These few articles, together with a pane of glass, constitute the most important accessories to Gloxinia culture in its first stage, if we do not take into account the rather indispensible elements of air, heat and water, without which the most sanguine horticulturist would hardly hope for success.

Sowing in February or March is recommended for the greenhouse, but I would advise those who wish to try window culture not to sow until the cold weather is well over, unless they are sure that they have facilities for preserving an even warm temperature for their experiments, and this is rarely possible in the dwelling house, as I find to my cost. Therefore, I think, under these circumstances, it is best not to sow until the last of April or first of May. There is little to be gained by sowing earlier, as plants from seed sown at this season have ample time to mature strong flowering bulbs for the next year.

To return to our subject. Having sifted the mold or earth to remove any coarse particles, fill the box within half an inch of the top with it, and press it down as firmly as possible, leaving an even surface. Set the box in a pan containing tepid water, and let it remain until the soil is thoroughly saturated, then remove and allow any superfluous water to drain off. Afterwards scatter the seeds thinly over the surface and sift a little fine earth over them through a sieve or coarse piece of muslin; cover the box with the pane of glass and set it in a warm place to await the process of germination. If in the greenhouse this is easily managed, but if in the dwelling house a shelf near the stove or a warm window will do nicely. I have even found the reservoir of my kitchen stove an acquisition for furnishing bottom heat to struggling plants. In case of using a reservoir for this purpose it is well to put a bit of board under your box, as a non-conductor, in event of too much heat. Give air frequently to prevent mould, and, should water be necessary before the plants are up, set the box again in a little warm water until the moisture appears on the surface of the soil. As soon as the seedlings are nicely up remove the glass and place the box in some warm location, where the plants may have the benefit of both light and air to prevent them from becoming drawn, and continue watering as before until they attain the dignity of from three to five leaves, when it is time to transplant each one to a small pot of rich, mellow earth, or several may be set in a larger pot and allowed to remain until they attain the height of an inch or so, when they may be transplanted to four-inch pots, and a few weeks later to six-inch pots, where they are to be left to complete their growth of the first year. Water as often as the earth becomes dry, but be sure that your pots are well drained, as, though the Gloxinia will endure a great deal of neglect in the matter of applying water, a deluge was not more fatal to the antediluvians than it will prove to this pretty flower. Stagnant water soon destroys the bulb beyond remedy. Do not place your plants, especially during the blooming period, in the direct rays of the summer sun, or they will be apt to droop and become limp, pitiable objects; but give them a little protection and they will reward you well for the trouble. They will do nicely with plenty of light, and little, if any, sunshine, and are therefore, to be recommended for those who have windows on the north or east side of the house.

GLOXINIA—UPRIGHT FLOWER.

While those who sow seed in the greenhouse may possibly be rewarded with a few flowers the first season, it is well for those who grow them under the disadvantage of the dry air and unequal temperature of the living-room not to expect any until the second year, or disappointment will likely result. Allow your young plants to grow until the tops show signs of ripening off, or till late in the autumn, if they seem inclined to do so, then gradually withhold water and put them, after the foliage is well dried off, beneath the staging, if in the greenhouse, or, if under house culture, in some warm and comparatively dry place where there is no danger of frost through the winter. I have a box which, covered with cretonne, presents quite a respectable appearance in the sitting-room and at the same time serves as a receptacle for my dormant plants until such a time as their starting shoots or my own convenience decides me to place them in the window again. One method of preserving the roots during the period of rest is packing them in sand, but I feel more certain of success if I allow them to remain undisturbed in the pots in which they were grown, for experience warns me to be careful how I meddle with dormant bulbs, although the growing plants can be repotted at any time, and even subjected to very rough treatment without much injury.

GLOXINIA—NODDING FLOWER.

When the Gloxinias show signs in the spring of waking from their long sleep into active life by the putting out of sundry pink or green shoots, remove them from their resting place to a warm window, and water carefully, but not too freely, until the foliage is well out: then take the plants up and shake the earth out of their roots, repotting into six or seven-inch pots, and using very rich, mellow earth or the compost usually recommended for house plants now set the plants in the window where they are to bloom. Always be careful not to over water for some time after repotting, as when the roots have been recently disturbed they are not in condition to take up water as when well established in the soil. Do not spot the leaves or blast the flower buds by getting them wet, but pour the water directly on the surface of the earth, using sufficient to penetrate to the bottom of the pot and thoroughly wetting the contents. It is far better to water thoroughly and only when necessary than to keep up a constant irrigation and I might add irritation, of the surface of the soil with homœopathic doses of water, leaving the roots deep down in the pot to shrivel and die from starvation, or rather, of thirst, while you indulge in the "pleasant fiction" of watering your plants once or twice every day. The old saying, "What is worth doing at all is worth doing well," applies very nicely to even the simple operation of watering a plant.

It is an easy matter to keep the Gloxinia in bloom from May until October or November, by starting the plants into growth "in succession." The buds usually appear, under favorable circumstances, the second season as soon as the plants have put forth a few leaves, and the flowers often remain a week or more before falling off, thus adding another good point to the many already scored in the favor of this beautiful exotic. The Geranium is looked upon as the plant which "suffereth all things, endureth all things," and generally fulfils any expectations in that respect, but after a long experience I can recommend the Gloxinia to plant-lovers as being nearly, if not quite, as easy of cultivation as this well known flower, while, in addition to this, its waxen bells, with their colors gorgeous as the plumage of a tropical bird, or delicate as an artist's dream, proclaim it as one of the aristocracy of the floral kingdom.

THE CINERARIA.

A few years ago the Cineraria was one of our most popular winter blooming plants, but since Roses, Carnations and other winter bloomers have taken its place its cultivation has been sadly neglected. But within the past year or two it has begun to occupy its proper place among choice winter blooming plants, and magnificent specimens are frequently seen at the horticultural exhibitions.

The Cineraria is generally considered to be a difficult plant to grow, but such is not the case, for, if its requirements are understood, no plant can be more easily grown. The mistakes generally consist in growing the plants in too warm a temperature instead of a cool one, and in overpotting the plants while small.

The seeds can be sown at almost any season of the year, but for the amateur cultivator the best time is from the middle of April until the middle of June. Indeed it is best to make two sowings, one about the end of April and the other about the tenth of June, but if only one sowing can be made it should be done about the middle of May, for the seed will vegetate much better if sown before hot weather sets in. The seed should be sown in well drained pots or pans filled with light, rich soil; sow very thinly and cover slightly, a mere dusting with a little compost will be sufficient, and press it down rather firmly with the bottom of a pot. If the seed is sown in April the pans should be placed in a warm, moist situation, close to the glass, and as soon as the young plants are large enough to handle they should be transplanted into other pans similarly prepared, and placed an inch and a half apart. These plants should be kept close and moist until growth commences, and by this time the weather will be warm enough to permit them to be removed to a cold-frame and treated as advised for the later sowing.

The later sowing should be made about the middle of May, and the seed-pans or pots removed to the cold-frame where they should be kept close and moist until the young plants are well up. As soon as they are strong enough to handle they should be transferred to other seed-pans, and placed about an inch and a half apart each way. It is best to keep the young plants close and moist until growth commences, when a little air should be given. The plants can be grown in the seed-pans until they commence to touch each other, and then they must be carefully taken up and potted into three-inch pots. When first potted water thoroughly and replace in the cold-frame as close together as possible, but on no account should the plants be allowed to touch each other.

Keep the young plants growing in a healthy condition, and as the pots become moderately filled with roots they should be shifted into pots about two sizes larger, and treated precisely as advised for the first potting.

This treatment should be continued throughout the summer and until the approach of cold weather, when they should be brought inside. If specimens are wanted the repotting should be continued until the plants are in pots from eight to ten inches in diameter.

When brought inside, the plants should be placed by themselves in the coolest part of the greenhouse, but keep them far enough apart to prevent the leaves in one pot from touching those in the next, and as soon as the flower-stalks make their appearance give the plants liquid manure water at least twice a week.

CINERARIA.

The cold-frame in which the plants are to be grown during the summer season should be placed on a bed of coal ashes in a partially shaded situation. The sash should also be given a light coat of whitewash, in order to keep the sun's rays from the plants, for, although the Cineraria likes to be grown in a light situation, yet it soon suffers if it is permitted to be exposed to the sun during the summer months, especially if it should happen to become a little dry at the roots. In this frame, and on the bed of ashes, the plants should be placed as closely together as possible, without the leaves of one plant being permitted to touch those of another from the time they are taken from the seed-pans until their period of blooming is past.

In potting, porous or soft-baked pots should always be used, and

THE CINERARIA.

see to it that they are well drained, as this is a very important point. In draining place a large piece of broken pot over the hole, then several smaller, and gradually fill up with smaller pieces until the pot is one-third filled; over this place a layer of moss, to prevent the soil from falling through.

The soil most suitable for the Cineraria is one composed of two-thirds turfy loam, one-third well decayed cow manure, with a fair sprinkling of bone-dust; mix thoroughly, and use the compost rough, pressing it down firmly around the plants.

The Cineraria is very subject to attacks of the aphis or green fly and the red spider. The latter can be prevented by growing the plants in a moist, cool atmosphere. The former is more troublesome, and requires constant watching, but a few leaves or stems of Tobacco scattered among the plants of the cold-frame, and renewed occasionally will keep them in subjection. In the greenhouse they can be destroyed by a slight fumigation of Tobacco. Water should be given thoroughly whenever necessary, and when the flower-stalks make their appearance give liquid manure water at least twice a week. Never permit the plants to suffer for water at any time, and keep them in a moist and cool atmosphere at all times, excepting in the winter, when the foliage should be kept rather dry in order to guard against damp, as this would soon destroy the foliage and thus materially injure the appearance of the plants.

A packet or two of seeds of the mixed varieties will produce a quantity of plants, and give a varied and beautiful display, but my experience with the double varieties has been anything but satisfactory.

It appears to be scarcely necessary for me to add that the plants are worthless and should be thrown away after the flowering season is past.

ANNUALS IN THE WINTER WINDOW-GARDEN.

What annuals can be satisfactorily raised in the winter window-garden, and how are they best managed?

Eight or ten years ago I began experimenting with annuals in the house in winter, sometimes only from curiosity, and because they gave interest and variety to the work, and I find those in the following list can be very safely recommended: Alyssum and Mignonette for fragrance; Petunias, Schizanthus, Asters, Balsams and Mimulus for their free-flowering qualities, and Browallia, Lobelia and Ageratum for blue colors. The following are also very good: Candytuft, Canna, Vinca, Stock, Mesembryanthemum, Alonsoa, Salvia, Phlox, Portulaca and Mimosa. For climbers there are Cobœa, Maurandya, both excellent, Ipomœa, Thunbergia, Cardiospermum and Tropæolum, all but the first mentioned suitable for baskets. Many coarse annuals, too, can be flowered in the window, though it is not advisable to give them room often. When the requisite coolness and humidity of air can be secured, we may have some of our little moisture-loving favorites, such as Whitlavia, Nemophila, and even the Pansy.

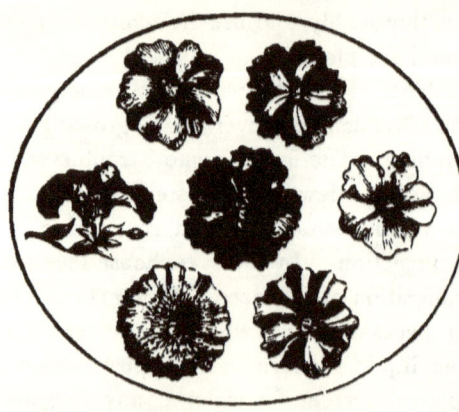

PETUNIAS IN VARIETY.

How are they best managed? In starting seeds and cuttings, or in dotting plants, I am always careful to have good drainage, generally using charcoal, for it is convenient, and helps to keep the soil in the pots sweet. A good rich soil, free from insects, and made light with a fourth part sand, and a little leaf-mold, agrees with most plants. Cuttings that root easily, such as those of Petunia, Browallia, Ageratum, &c., I insert firmly in a pot of very sandy soil, water well and place in a sheltered corner of the veranda, where they are shielded from the strong winds and the hot noon-day sun, but get the morning sunshine; keeping the soil moist they root in a very few days.

ANNUALS IN THE WINTER WINDOW-GARDEN.

Seeds of Sweet Alyssum I start the last of August. From hree to six young plants can be started in a good sized pot. A good light is needed while the plants are young, but after flowering much sunlight is not required. Alyssum is good for baskets, but mine are drooping from a bracket on a level with my face, that I may the more conveniently inhale their fragrance, so like the sweetness of the wee white Violets I used to gather from the sunny knolls in the old orchard.

Ageratum I prefer to grow from cuttings, but young seedlings do equally well. I take cuttings from flowering plants in the garden about the middle of summer, and pot for the house after they are well rooted; they are loaded with flowers all winter. Once I neglected to take cuttings at the right time, but had plants on the veranda that had been blooming in pots all summer. I cut them back severely; they rapidly made a new growth and bloomed well, but not so freely as those grown from cuttings.

Alonsoa will please those who like small, bright flowers. Young plants can be potted in the fall, and with care, if kept rather warm, will flower well.

Aster seeds can be sown late in the spring, or in June, and the young plants transplanted several times; this will cause them to be "stocky," and to have good roots. Give a rich soil and plenty of room in a cool place. If the weather is dry, water and mulch. Thus treated, handsome specimens may be obtained, which may be taken up in the fall when in blossom. Place each plant in a pot just large enough to hold it easily, and remove to a cool situation in the house.

Browallia seeds can be started in the summer, and the plants raised in pots, and brought along in the cold frame, if this convenience is possessed. As the plants grow, pinch them back occasionally, don't neglect it, and they will branch out generously, and be in good condition to take into the house in the fall. Use some leaf-mold in the soil. I prefer to raise the plants from cuttings. A fair amount of sun, warmth and water seems to suit them. They brighten my window all winter with their cheerful and abundant blue and white flowers. The green aphis loves the Browallia. I look for him if I see a leaf turning brown. He is easily smoked out without harm to the plant.

Young Balsam plants can be potted when two inches high, shifting as needed to a size larger pot; but the best way is to take cuttings from the side branches of the best varieties, about the first of

August. When potted for the house, give a rich soil and a good light. After the blossoms are well developed they are more enduring if kept somewhat cool.

Any of the Calendulas or Marigolds will blossom in the house, if one cares to give them room.

Candytuft is beautiful in a hanging basket. The white is the prettiest. With good soil and treatment it will bloom long and abundantly in the winter. Seeds can be sown directly in the receptacle in which it is desired that they should flower, if preferred.

Centaurea Cyanus; I once transferred a few thrifty young plants of Bachelor's Button from the garden to the house, in autumn, and every one was surprised and interested to see them blooming freely in the winter beside my choice greenhouse plants.

Canna is one of the few things that will bear to be taken up roughly, and brought forward to the heat and light without ceremony. I generally take two large pots, just alike, plant a clump of dark variety in one, and one of light ones in the other. Placed each side of the window they match well and give the winter garden a tropical aspect. Cannas will flourish, blossom, and even ripen their seeds in the winter, if their quarters are warm and sunny. When the old stalks are done blooming, they can be cut away, giving room to the younger shoots, which will bloom in their turn; when they, also, can be cut away, giving place to the fresher stalks that are constantly springing from the roots of the plant.

Celosia; young plants can be taken care of in pots during the summer, or plants can be lifted from the garden and removed to the window.

I once saw a plant of Cleome in a window, and it was quite a handsome bush.

I have beeen unable to improve upon my first experience in starting Cobœa seeds. In March I planted them, edgewise in a well-drained box of very light sandy soil. The earth was moist, so I did not water any, but dipped a flannel cloth in water, wrung it, and wrapped the whole box in it, and placed it behind the sitting-room stove. As often as the cloth became dry, I repeated the operation, watching closely until I knew the seeds had sprouted by the earth being lifted in little places in the box. Then I dispensed with the cloth, and immediately placed the box in a warm, sunny window. In a few hours the lubberly young plants lifted, and were helping themselves to their first meal of sunshine. When they were about four inches high, I potted one of the best in an eight or ten-

ANNUALS IN THE WINTER WINDOW-GARDEN. 19

inch pot, giving support. When four or five feet high I transplanted it to one end of a large window box, which was furnished with other plants, a high arched trellis and castors. I kept it on the veranda through the summer, then it was removed to the window, where it bloomed long and continuously. In using large boxes for flowering plants, I improvise partitions, so that the roots of each plant may have no more room than it needs. I place shingles or thin boards, edgewise in the box. The earth will hold them in place. This causes the plants to flower very freely. The Cobœa requires a rich soil, plenty of room, warmth, sunshine and water. I start Cobœa cuttings in sand, under glass, and sometimes propagate them by layering, cutting a notch near a joint.

MORNING GLORY.

Convolvulus; If I could afford nothing but Morning Glories, I would still have a gay window garden. One came up by chance in my window, and bloomed finely. Convolvulus minor is beautiful in baskets, the flowers looking as delicate as soap bubbles.

Cardiospermum seeds grow easily, if started in a warm place. The plant grows fast, and is a pretty vine for the house, but will not bear getting chilled. With me it is troubled with the aphis, but he is easily smoked out.

Dianthus can be flowered in the house, but winter Carnations are so much nicer that it hardly pays.

Fenzlia is a little jewel in pots or mixed baskets.

Ipomœas are nice in pots with trellis, or baskets. They require considerable heat. I. coccinea will run above the windows in winter.

Leptosiphon is delicate and pretty in pots or baskets. Give it a light soil and a cool place.

Linum; this airy and graceful flower is quite pretty in mixed baskets. I never tried any but the red in winter.

The trailing annual Lobelias are valuable for winter use, especially suitable in small baskets. Seeds start readily in a light rich soil, and even young plants, if given good light, grow fast in the winter garden and bloom freely. The deep, rich blue is very lovely grown in the same pot with Alyssum.

For winter use seeds of Maurandya can be started late, but I prefer to take cuttings from the veranda or in the garden. The fine branches, with their delicate but abundant foliage and beautiful flowers, should be allowed to droop, or run up the wires of the basket and loop and twist about in their own graceful way. A rich, light soil, warmth and sunshine suit it.

Mignonette one should never be without, for it can be grown at any time. Its perfume reminds me of the delicious fragrance of freshly gathered red Raspberries. Sow seeds the last of August. It will droop if you prefer it to; it is a good companion to Alyssum. With these two sweet little flowers, and a few small Rose Geranium leaves, worn in the corsage or the hair, no jewelry is needed, and in contrast with their fragrance, the most costly perfume is gross.

Mesembryanthemums are easily grown from the seeds. They are adapted to baskets. Care must be taken not to break their tender branches. I am careful to give them fresh air to prevent their damping off, as they sometimes do if they are kept too warm and moist without air; still they will not do well in a chilly room.

Mimulus is an excellent winter bloomer; healthy, and requiring only good, fair care. Its branches are tender, and care should be taken not to break them. It is a nice basket plant. M. moschatus, yellow, though not quite as pretty as some varieties, is interesting on account of its musky fragrance.

Nolana is a good basket plant. For winter use seeds can be sown in July. It transplants easily, does best in a light, sandy soil. Flowes resemble those of Convolvulus minor, but are more solid, and close in the afternoon.

Nemophila is one of the loveliest little flowers when well grown. It has fern-like foliage and perfect form. If seeds are sown late, we may have them in winter, if a cool place and humid air can be secured.

If Nierembergia seeds are sown late in the summer and the young plants transplanted to a basket, they will give their graceful flowers in the winter.

ANNUALS IN THE WINTER WINDOW-GARDEN. 21

Phacelia makes a charming pot plant, not so much on account of its neat little flowers as for its abundant fern-like foliage and beautiful form. It must be well watered, and needs a cool, moist place, but is not so particular in this respect as Nemophila. I have only tried the blue Phacelia.

Portulaca: it is well to fill a pot or basket with cuttings about the last of August, for they root quickly and bloom well in the house in winter.

I love Pansies so well that I always try to find a place to suit them. I have a large, well ventilated, mouse-proof cellar, well lighted by double glass windows. On the broad ledge of the south window, I sometimes place a box of Pansies, and sometimes Nemophila and Whitlavia, and they do the best there of any place I ever tried. Last summer, I found I could start Whitlavia from slips, for I did in July.

Perilla is quite serviceable as a foliage plant for the house, if one has nothing better. The leaves of my variety have a strong, peculiar, but pleasant scent.

The Petunia is something of solid worth. I used to take the late plants from the garden, that had not bloomed, looking as though they were ready to do the best of service, but with the best of care they would never bloom till toward spring. The right way every time is to take slips. A year ago last July I started a box of cuttings of the best single varieties in my garden. They rooted nicely, and I planted five in a box fifteen inches long by nine inches wide, placing one plant in the middle and one in each corner. The rest I gave each a pot by itself. Supports were given, as they always should be to all plants that need it, keeping the plants in good shape. The first of October they began blooming, and oh, what a wealth of blossoms those Petunias gave for ten months. All through the dead of winter there were from two hundred and fifty to three hundred blossoms, which hung in wreaths—white, red, striped and blotched—in that box alone, besides hundreds of buds just opening. And the foliage as beautiful as that of a Heliotrope, was thick and green, drooping over the box, completely hiding the soil and supports. I use soot-water quite freely on all my plants, for I am certain that it helps to keep the lower foliage bright. Petunias like sunshine and plenty of warmth. They need more warmth to produce flowers than to produce leaves. This winter I have them in hanging baskets.

Phlox will bloom gaily in the winter garden, and young plants can be grown in summer for this purpose. Give them fresh air, and do not crowd them too much, or they will mildew.

Sensitive Plant; start seeds under glass, and pot one of the best of the young plants, plunging the pot in the earth, after the weather is warm, transferring it to the house in the fall.

TROPÆOLUM.

Ten Weeks Stocks, for winter use, I would prefer to raise from seeds sown late in the season, if it were not for the danger of the plants proving to bear single flowers, and single Stocks are worthless. So I go to the garden, when the character of the plant is determined, and very carefully take up the best of the most backward, and pot them in rich soil, plunging the pots in a cool place, keeping watered if the weather is dry. When removed to the house keep cool and moist.

Seeds of the Schizanthus sown in July or August, in light, rich soil, will give plants that will bloom in winter; but, for earlier use, old plants may be removed from the garden to the house.

Thunbergia seeds germinate easily if kept warm and moist, either in the house or later in the open ground. I place the eye of the seed downward. Pots with young plants may be plunged during the summer, that is, buried in the earth to the rim of the pot. Give the vines support early and pinch occasionally. Or, cuttings may be taken from the plants in the garden. The red spider sometimes attacks it, but has never troubled me. T. alata grows from twelve to fifteen feet high here in the open ground. I think T. Bakeri is the prettiest.

Tropæolum Lobbianum is easily grown from seeds or cuttings.

ANNUALS IN THE WINTER WINDOW-GARDEN.

It is free from insects, and fine for pots or baskets. I always take especial pains with the drainage, and have the soil such as water will readily perforate, or they will sometimes drop their lower leaves, which ruins the appearance of any plant to me. A too heavy soil is, in effect, only another style of bad drainage. With me, a somewhat cool, moist air and even temperature suit it best.

I have also experimented with Euphorbia, Mirabilis, and others, with indifferent success. I intend to try them again. In conclusion, I would say to all: Grow flowers, "love truth, love GOD, love virtue, and be happy."

WINTER SUPPLY OF VIOLETS AND PANSIES.

How can am. ·urs without greenhouses keep up a winter supply of Violets and Pansies?

To grow Violets in winter outside of a greenhouse, is considered by practical gardeners one of the easiest things to perform. Many florists keep them in cold-frames exclusively, for, as a rule, they have not room for them in their greenhouses, unless a house is built on purpose for them. They may be grown in pots, as window plants, provided plenty of air can be given on sunny days, and a steady temperature between 35° and 55° can be kept up. If kept in too high an artificial temperature they will not flower much, but will make up in red spider what they lack in blossom. A Geranium, a Carnation and a Monthly Rose may be wintered and flowered at a low temperature, if plenty of sunlight prevails. An occasional little frost will not hurt the Geranium : the Carnation can bear considerable frost, and the Rose is the hardiest of them all. Yet all these three named plants will do admirably in an average temperature of 60°. With the Violet it is different, and it wants to be kept cool at all times, if it is expected that it will fulfill its mission. All this does not imply that the temperature of a Violet house or frame should never be allowed to run up to 60°, because sometimes the heat in the day time is not always under control. The sun may sometimes make the atmosphere under glass warmer than the gardener would like to have it, but to raise the sash only one inch would let the frost in and do more damage than the heat. In such a case a little too high temperature is the least evil.

A good place to grow Violets may be constructed at the south side of a dwelling. Dig a pit two feet deep along the house. Into this put a stout frame to receive common hot-bed sash, the sash to lean against the building. Tear down the wall that separates the frame from the cellar under the house, and put a row of windows in its place. The idea of this is, that the natural heat in the cellar shall keep your Violet frame at a steady temperature. At the same time you may work over your flowers, no matter what the outside weather may be, and when no air can be given from the outside, it may be done indirectly inside. When the outside sash is open, the inside may be shut. Thus the sun will warm up the cellar, and perhaps store a little heat for the night. Is your cellar already

WINTER SUPPLY OF VIOLETS AND PANSIES.

warmed up by a furnace? If it is, then I am sorry, but even in that case, we can regulate the temperature by having the inside sash open but a little; or, perhaps the furnace heat will save the trouble of covering up nights. Keep your eye on the thermometer, and by a little watching you will soon learn what to do. I said dig a pit two feet deep. This must be filled in again to the depth of one foot with some good garden loam, well composted with stable manure, well rotted, thus making the Violet bed about one foot lower than the surface of the ground outside. There are, however, houses where a frame like the one described would be an architectural impossibility, or the owner might object to having his house disfigured in such a manner. In such cases we must resort to the common cold-frame. A simple frame, made of heavy plank, settled in the ground, covered with hot-bed sash and protected with straw mats and shutters, will keep Violets well. There is, however, a great drawback to such frames, and that is, that there may be times when you would like to pick a bunch of flowers out of them, but cannot get at them on account of too cold weather. There may be plenty of them there, they smile at you, or perhaps mock you through the glass, but to raise the sash for only two minutes would soon set their smiles to rest, and yours as well, for that matter.

I will here describe a frame that will not only remove these obstacles, but at the same time be perfectly sae from frost, which is not always the case with the common cold-frame, not even with the heaviest covering. Select a space with a southern exposure, and dig a pit six feet deep, it may be deeper, or not quite so deep, according to locality. I choose six feet because it is a convenient depth to walk upright in. The length and width must be governed by the size and number of your sash, but as the size commonly used is three feet by six, we will take that as our standard. This would make our pit a little less than six feet wide, making allowance for pitch of the sash. Board up this pit inside, to keep the earth from caving. The boarding will terminate in the frame to take the sash. Inside of this structure build a table three and one-half feet wide, such as you see in most greenhouses, and two and one-half feet from its highest point. I allow one foot slant for a six-foot sash. You will find a bench three and one-half feet wide about as wide as you care to reach across. It leaves a space over two feet in width for a walk. A still better plan would be to make the bench six inches narrower, and leaving that space behind for the air to circulate through.

But how are you going to get into it? To do that you must sacrifice the space of one sash, or rather make your pit and frame three feet longer than you have sash to put on. This space must be partitioned off from the rest of the pit and a door put in opposite the walk. Next, put in some stairs and cover the whole tightly with heavy boards, leaving a hole for a trap-door, just large enough to let you through conveniently. You may call this part an entry, ante-room, hallway, vestibule, or anything you please. Once inside this structure, the world is shut off from you; you are separated from its distinctions and its cares. Left alone with your flowers, over your head the winds may roar and the snowflakes may fall, you will mind them not, for you are in a world entirely your own. But I am going too fast, for as yet our frame has nothing to show but bare boards.

The principle on which a pit like this works is, that it is dug out far beyond the frost line. The heat radiating from this large surface of unfrozen earth is sufficient to keep Jack Frost at bay, and that is all the heat a Violet or Pansy requires to live and thrive.

In localities where there is much zero weather it would be well to remove the earth around the frame to the depth of two feet, and three feet wide. This cavity to be filled with leaves, litter and fresh horse manure well trodden down. In any case the glass must

WINTER SUPPLY OF VIOLETS AND PANSIES. 27

be covered in severe nights with straw mats or shutters, or both. And now let us take the more pleasant topic: The cultivation of the Violet.

The varieties mostly cultivated for winter flowering are the Neapolitan, a light blue, double one, and Marie Louise, a dark blue and also double. Both are varieties of the so-called English Violet, Viola odorata. They are propagated by cuttings, or by dividing the old plants. The latter is the better method for amateurs. The best time to do this is the month of April, when the old plants are through flowering, and as soon as the ground is in good working order, so that the divided plants can be set out in the open ground at once, where they are to remain during summer. This must be repeated every spring. Select only the best and throw the rest away or give to some friend, it will not do to set out the whole clumps of old plants. During the hot months of summer they will not grow much, they are children of a temperate climate. It is well to give them some protection. Some let weeds grow over them for the sake of shade, but to let weeds grow is against the true principles of gardening, and if Violets do better under the protection of other plants, why not mix them with cultivated ones? I plant mine in the same rows with Carnations that are intended for winter-flowering, planting a Violet and Carnation alternately. Nothing needs to be done to them during summer, besides weeding and cutting off the runners, until they are to be removed to winter quarters.

In about the month of September prepare the bed that is to receive your Violets. If a solid bed, as in the frame first described, the soil should be from ten inches to a foot deep; if a raised bench, five or six inches will be sufficient. The soil must be rich, and, if possible, of a nature to retain moisture. After the bed is prepared plant the Violets in rows across the bench. The rows to be a foot apart and as many plants in the row as you can get in without crowding them too much. Water them well with a sprinkler to settle the earth around the roots, and give them partial shade, but no glass yet. When the plants show signs of growth, gradually remove the shade and give them a thorough soaking with soapsuds warm from the wash-tub. Put on the glass when frost threatens. Ventilate whenever the weather permits, and on very mild days remove the glass entirely, or at least every other sash. Keep them free from weeds, cut off all runners and carefully remove all mouldy and rotten leaves. Water freely whenever the surface of the soil shows indications of dryness, but without wetting the foliage. To bring the flowers to the greatest perfection there is nothing better than soapsuds applied about once a month. But never do any kind of watering unless the ground asks for it by the dry appearance of its surface. I have allowed my Violets to go for two months without water.

Pansies require about the same winter treatment as Violets, only give them the sunniest place in the frame. Sow your seeds in the beginning of August, in a cool situation. Sow plenty of it, because the plants will not all be good for winter flowering. When the young seedlings are large enough to be handled, prick them out in a prepared border of good rich soil, about four inches apart, and keep them well watered. In the first week of October they should have fairly begun to flower. Select only the best for winter blooming, and do not plant any in your frame that has not shown at least one flower, for after the first flower more are sure to follow. After having your bed planted to your own satisfaction, give it all the care you can, after the rules above given, and an abundance of flowers will be your reward.

How can the finest pot-plants of Chrysanthemums be raised, and what varieties are desirable?

Young cuttings of this popular fall-flowering plant should be rooted in sand, in greenhouse, with a gentle bottom heat, any time from the third week in February to the middle of March. About the first of April the rooted cuttings should be potted into three-inch pots, using any common garden soil. Those who do not have the convenience of a greenhouse, yet have the roots of last year's plants, which have been kept through the winter in boxes of soil in a light cellar, or protected in a cold-frame, should, about the first of

April, divide the roots, putting a small piece of the root and shoots into a three-inch pot, the same as a rooted cutting. Water moderately at first, and keep the plants in the house or under glass. Three or four weeks after this all should be repotted into four-inch pots, adding rather richer soil, and water as they need, and pinch out the top shoots to form them into good shape.

The next shift should be into six-inch pots, using good, rich soil, and about the middle of May plunge the pots into the ground, nearly up to the rim, about eighteen inches apart, in that part of the garden facing to the southeast, giving more water if the weather should be dry and warm. Also give them weak liquid manure occasionally, and stop, or pinch off, the shoots to make them bushy. They can be raised to a single stem or bushy down to the soil, according to the grower's fancy. Having tried both, I prefer the latter method.

To obtain good, large, healthy plants, the last shifting should be made into eight or ten-inch pots, adding the best rich soil made from old, well-rotted cow manure, or from old hot-beds. This last potting into their blooming pots should not be later than the second week in June, sinking the pots a little deeper in the ground, and two feet apart. The pinching off the top shoots must not be neglected, as they grow rapidly about this time; this may be done from time to time until about the last week in July, after which time they should be let grow to form their flowering buds, staking and tying out as they may require. Special attention must be given to watering; through the hot, dry weather of July and August they must be thoroughly watered at least twice every day, except in case the weather should be showery, and in extreme hot, dry winds even three times a day would be better. It will also be very beneficial to them, when the buds begin to form, to give them a good soaking with guano water twice a week. One large tablespoonful to two gallons of soft water will be strong enough; if this should be too offensive to the smell, the same proportion of Bowker's Flower Food can be used.

It is a very good plan to mulch the top of the pots with coarse, rotted cow manure; it will prevent the soil from getting hard in the pots from continual watering, also keep the roots cool. The pots should remain in the ground until the nights get cold, when they should be lifted to the surface, placed securely so that they will not be blown down by wind or storm, thus being ready to be lifted into shelter when there is danger of frost.

The insects known as the black aphides are very fond of these plants, fixing themselves generally around the young shoots and flowering buds. The most effecctive way to get rid of them is to get a quarter or half pound of fine tobacco dust, sprinkle it with the thumb and fingers on the tops of the plants after rain, or after being watered; most of the insects will step down or fall down, and the few that remain can be washed off in watering. As often as the insects return give them the same reception, so that they will not have time to damage the buds or plants.

To decide what varieties are best for pot plants is the most difficult task, so many new and valuable ones being introduced every year. There are three classes of Chrysanthemums, viz.: Japanese, Chinese and Pompon. The first has ragged and fringed, large, loose flowers. One of the very best of this class is La Frisure, being dwarf, very early, large flower much fringed, light blush color, changing to nearly white; Elaine, Lady Selborne and Mrs. Charles Cary are all splendid, and pure white; Golden Dragon, twisted petals, large and good, golden yellow; Grandiflorum, very large, one of the very best, golden yellow; Hackney Holmes, splendid, bright crimson, tipped with gold; Rex rubrorum, rich crimson; Rosea superba, lilac rose, tipped with buff, large and good; Nuit d'Hiver, dwarf and free, bronze and brown, tipped with gold; Rubra striata, rosy salmon, very pretty.

Chinese varieties—Mrs. George Rundell, one of the very best in cultivation, pure white, incurved; Spotless, large and good, pure white; Webb's Queen, large and good, blush white; Golden Empress, very fine, primrose yellow, incurved; Jardin des Plantes, golden yellow, good; Lady Talfourd, delicate rose-lilac, splendid, incurved; Prince of Wales, rich violet-plum, very fine; President Wilder, large, crimson, tipped with gold, yellow button in center, very fine; Duchess of Connaught, large and finely incurved, splendid form, silver blush; Felicity, flowers large and fine, cream color, late.

Pompon varieties—Arbre de Noel, compact and good, bronze and chrome; Bob and Fanny, both red and good, the latter late; Madamoiselle Marthe, flowers in large clusters, very fine, pure white; Montgolfier, beautiful, maroon, tipped with gold; Salamon, rich violet-plum; Model of Perfection, lilac and white; General Canrobert, fine and early, pure yellow; Souvenir de Jersey, small, good, golden yellow, late; La Vierge, large, pure white; Perle des Beauties, large and good, rich amaranth purple.

The above are all good and quite reliable varieties. There are many others not named in this list that are very good, but most of the above varieties have been proved and found to be some of the very best. I find that many of the new varieties are not as hardy as some of the older kinds, especially some of the Japanese varieties lately introduced. Therefore it is necessary that these should be grown in pots, so that they can easily be taken into the house to prevent injury from early frosts.

As there is quite a difference between the early and late varieties, all who love these popular and beautiful late autumn flowers can enjoy their beauty from the first of November until Christmas or New Years day.

THE CALCEOLARIA.

When well grown, the herbaceous Calceolarias are very beautiful, and a few years ago they were among the most popular winter blooming plants; but unfortunately they were crowded aside by other plants, and for several years their merits remained unnoticed; of late they are beginning to receive more attention.

They are, by many, considered rather difficult to cultivate, but such is not the case if their requirements are understood. The mistakes in their culture consist in growing them in too high a temperature instead of a cool one, in over-potting and over-watering the plants while small, and by so doing materially injuring their health and vigor of growth, thus rendering them liable to the attacks of numerous insect pests.

The best time for sowing the seed is from the middle of May to the middle of June, for it will vegetate much better if sown before the hot weather sets in.

In order to cultivate the Calceolaria readily and successfully a cold-frame will be found to be absolutely necessary; this should be placed on a bed of coal ashes, in a partially shaded situation, and the sash whitewashed or painted, so as to shield the plants from the hot sun. The sash can be raised or closed as may be necessary to protect the plants from severe storms and sudden changes in temperature.

The seed should be sown in a well drained pot or pan, filled with light, loamy soil; sow it very thinly and press into the earth with the bottom of a pot. Place the pot or pan in the cold-frame, and keep it rather close until the young plants make their appearance. The soil in the pans should be dampened occasionally, but avoid keeping them too wet, as it may cause the young plants to damp off.

As soon as the plants are strong enough to handle, they should be transplanted into other pans similarly prepared, and placed about an inch and a half apart each way. These young plants should be carefully watered, and kept close and moist for a few days; but when they have taken root a little air should be given in order to prevent them from becoming drawn. As soon as the plants commence to touch each other they should be transplanted into three-inch pots filled with light rich soil, and be watered thoroughly, and then placed in the cold-frame as close together as possible, but the plants should not set so close as to touch each other. Keep the air rather close for a few days to enable them to take root, and afterwards give a little air day and night. As soon as the pots are fairly filled with roots, the plants should be shifted into pots two sizes larger, and treated precisely as before. This treatment should be continued through the entire summer and to the approach of cold weather, when the plants should be brought inside and placed in the coolest part of the green-house. If specimen plants are wanted, the repotting should be continued until the plants occupy eight or nine-inch pots. Never permit the leaves of one plant to touch those of another from the time the young plants make their appearance until they have ceased blooming.

CALCEOLARIAS.

Drainage is of the utmost importance; even the smallest sized pots should be one-third filled. In draining place a large piece of pot over the hole in the bottom of the pots, then around and above it place several smaller, and gradually use smaller pieces until the pot is one third filled, and over this place a layer of moss to prevent the soil from falling through.

The soil should be light and rich and composed of two-thirds well decayed sods, one-third well decomposed cow or sheep manure, with a fair sprinkling of bone dust and sharp sand. Mix thoroughly and use the compost rough. In potting press it down well around the plants.

The precise time of blooming of Calceolarias will depend greatly on the temperature and situation in which the plants are grown, and as they do best in a cool temperature they will not usually commence to bloom until the end of February or first of

THE CALCEOLARIA.

March, and they usually remain in bloom for a month or six weeks if the flowers are not permitted to become injured by damp. It is best to retard the flowering somewhat, for the flowers will be small and the plants will continue to bloom for a short time only, if forced into bloom.

The Calceolaria is very subject to the attacks of the red-spider and the green-fly. To avoid the spiders the plants at all times should be grown in a moist, cool atmosphere, but in the dark, dull days of winter be careful to guard against damp, which would soon destroy the foliage. The green-fly can be prevented by scattering a few leaves or stems of tobacco among the plants in the cold-frame and renewing them occasionally. In the greenhouse they should be given a slight fumigation of tobacco.

Every day the plants should be carefully examined and thoroughly watered, if necessary. It is of the highest importance in the successful cultivation of the Calceolaria to secure an uninterrupted growth from seed to bloom. To secure this the plants must be given a suitable soil, an ample supply of room for their roots, and they must be thoroughly watered whenever necessary. To do all this requires considerable care and attention, for a little neglect will almost ruin the plants. But no plant will much better repay the care and attention bestowed upon it than the Calceolaria.

THE CYCLAMEN.

What is the best method of treatment in the propagation and cultivation of the Cyclamen to secure fine blooming plants?

The genus Cyclamen is composed of some seven or eight species, and their several varieties. They are low plants, having very beautiful flowers and very prettily marked leaves. They are natives of Europe and Asia, some varieties being very abundant in Switzerland and Italy. Although some of the varieties are to be found in almost every greenhouse, yet the Cyclamen is too little known when we consider the ease with which it can be cultivated, and the length of time the flowers remain in perfection, the profusion of bloom, to say nothing of its great value for greenhouse and window garden decoration.

The plants are easily cultivated, doing best in a compost of two parts of well decayed sods, one of leaf-mold, or cow dung, and a little sharp sand. A sprinkling of soot thoroughly mixed with the soil will increase the size and brilliancy of the bloom. In potting, be sure to drain well, as good drainage is indispensible to success; if the pots are filled about one-third with drainage it is none too much. Use porous or soft-baked pots by all means, and let the size of the pot be determined by the size of the plant, remembering, as a rule, that Cyclamens do not require large pots. When first potted water thoroughly, afterwards more sparingly, until growth commences. When potted the plants can be placed in a cold-frame, in any sunny situation, from which the sashes can be removed on all favorable occasions, and water given as required. On the approach of cool weather they should be brought inside and placed in a light, sunny position where they can be given a winter temperature of from 40° to 50°. During growth and flowering water should be given as often as necessary, and liquid manure water at least twice a week. After their flowering season water should be gradually withheld, but do not permit them to become absolutely dry. About the first of May they can be planted out in a nicely prepared border, one having a northerly or easterly exposure being preferred. Place the plants about six inches apart each way, and let the bulbs or corms be placed at least two inches under gronnd. Keep them clear and free from weeds, and about the first of September they can be taken up and potted, as above advised. No watering is

THE CYCLAMEN.

required after they are planted out, but care is necessary to guard against mice, as they are very fond of the bulbs, and often destroy great numbers of them.

Propagation is readily effected by seeds, which should be sown about the first of February, in a pot or pan filled with a compost of light sandy soil. Sow thinly and cover very slightly, and place in a warm situation as close to the glass as possible. Keep moist until the young plants make their appearance, which will be in about three weeks, although it occasionally takes three months for some of the seeds to vegetate, so do not be impatient if the young plants do not appear at once. As soon as the seedlings are large enough to handle they should be transferred to thumb pots or else into seed-pans, placing them at least two inches apart; place these young plants in a situation similar to that in which the seed-pans were placed, and water very carefully, as to dry or drown them is equally injurious, and, as soon as they attain a larger size, they should be transferred into three-inch pots. In about eight or ten weeks some of them will be large enough to be transferred into four-inch pots, which is large enough to bloom them in, and treat the others similarly as soon as they are of sufficient size. If carefully treated the plants of all the species will be large enough to bloom in the fall, excepting Cyclamen Persicum and its varieties, which will begin to flower in January.

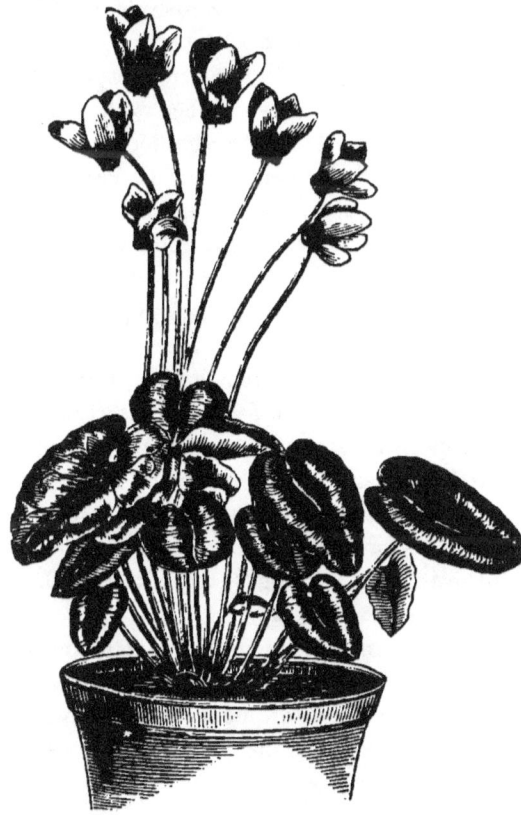

THE CYCLAMEN.

It will thus be seen that by sowing the seed early and keeping the plants growing during the summer, nice blooming plants are soon obtained. The best place for growing the young plants during the summer season is to take a cold-frame and place it on a bed of coal ashes in any partially shaded situation, and in the frame place the young plants. By the means of sashes the young plants can be protected from storms and rain, and they can be easily watered when necessary, and, besides, a part of the frame can be used for growing Primulas, Cinerarias, and Calceolarias, if not wanted for Cyclamens.

Of the several species, C. Europæum, pinkish-purple, and C. Europæum album, pure white, bloom from October to January, while the Ivy-leaved, C. hæderifolium, with its very large rosy-purple flowers blooms from September to January. When well grown these are extremely pretty plants, and it is to be regretted that they are so rarely seen in cultivation at the present time. C. Persicum, and its varieties, stand at the head of the family, and are the ones most generally cultivated; a packet or two of any good strain will give all sorts of different shades of color, from pure white to the deepest red and spotted. Of late there has been much improvement in the size and form of the flowers, and these varieties are offered under the names of C. Persicum grandiflorum and C. Persicum giganteum. The bulbs of this species are so flat and so nearly alike on each side that amateur cultivators are often puzzled to know which is the top. If carefully examined the remnants or scars of old leaf-stems will be seen, indicating the upper part, and it should be remembered that the corms or bulbs of Cyclamens are quite worthless after their third season of blooming, so that it is advisable to raise a few plants from seed every year.

The red spider is the only insect that troubles the Cyclamen, and as a remedy I advise dipping the leaves of the plant in soapy water every day from the time the insects are noticed until they are all destroyed, indeed, it is advisable to dip the plants twice a week as a preventive rather than a remedy.

THE ROSE AS A HOUSE PLANT.

How can the Rose be best managed as a house plant, and what varieties are most suitable for that purpose?

Many a Rose lover, discouraged by repeated failure, has gazed with envy upon the thriftiness of some old fashioned Rose, crimson with its wealth of half-double flowers. The uncultured mind, whose one success it is, cherishes it as a miracle of beauty, and so it is, in contrast to its barren surroundings and the battered tin pail, its abiding place. One who is obliged to dwell in a habitation barren of luxuries, and without works of art which are abhorrent of steam, and a "best room," which monopolizes south windows, but having a lined box for the night protection of plants, may delight in Roses with comparatively little trouble.

The power to command a conservatory ought also to command knowledge and appliances that will make work easy. I address my topic to the difficulties so much more numerous, that beset ordinary house culture, with its rooms papered and carpeted, and its cherished bric-a-brac.

All Rose culture must compass certain conditions; good soil, fresh and well tempered air, moisture and protection from all enemies, and, for abundant flowers southern sunlight. If you procure your plants growing in pots from the greenhouse, keep them by themselves for a while, giving them special care, until you are sure that no insects lurk among, and that they may not drop their foliage, through change of atmosphere. If your plants come by mail do not unpack until you can give them attention. Let them lie in tepid water while you prepare the pots. Nearly all florists direct us to place the plants in pots as small as possible, but, I think, in the dry air of the house, pots somewhat larger, with bits of charcoal, bone burnt or raw, and gravel for drainage, give better results.

You do well to exercise care in the soil for the Rose. For me, a mixture composed of rich clay in much the largest proportion, a little leaf-mold from the woods, aad soil from the grassy edge of a barnyard, the soil being very sandy, has proved best, though I have secured excellent growth from the latter alone, using larger pots in succession. Spread the roots naturally, sprinkle in the earth, pressing it firmly into place, shower, and set your plants, if possible, in an east kitchen window. Here steam and heat are more likely to accord with the treatment they have formerly received. Do not water again at the roots until dry, but sacrifice your window, giving the foliage, likewise the window, a fine, misty shower every afternoon until all is well. For this you may use a syringe or small whisk broom.

If there is the least hesitancy in growth, or the leaves droop, wash daily with a soft brush or feather, rinsing it constantly, and never using the water for a healthy plant after one that is drooping. If any flower buds start, remove them immediately, and cut back the plant promptly to the buds that show quick and thrifty growth.

After plants are growing where you wish them to bloom, they will need constant protection against the invasion of all enemies. I rid my plants of the aphis, etc., most effectually in the fall by destroying all the little flies that sport upon the window just at twilight, when the plants are first brought within. In fact, strict attention at an early stage of growth saves later a great deal of work in all directions. Yet be always vigilant, else the minute bud will disappear so quickly you will think yourself deceived, or the bud whose unfolding beauty you are ready to enjoy will turn to one side and refuse to open, while you may visit your disappointment upon the aphis, waxed corpulent at its base. Dipping the branches in weak tobacco water is an excellent preventive, but you may better enjoy the sweetness of your Roses by watchfulness.

The red spider, with me, is somewhat annoying. Immersing plants in water when small, and showering them when larger, will check the pest, or you may hold the plant firmly in position and rinse the tops in weak soap suds. I resort to my brush, washing stems most thoroughly, since by dislodging insects the new points of growth gain opportunity to start. You will find spiders most numerous at the back of the leaf at the base, and along the midvein, their webs being mostly upon the old growth and where overhanging leaves have afforded shelter. As you look through your plant to the light, remove gently the seeming particles of dust upon the new growth, making sure they have no life. Pick and burn all yellow or fallen leaves.

Against mildew, I find sufficient protection by rubbing flowers of sulphur upon the first leaf which shows infection, at the same time powdering plant and surface of the soil so lightly that it is scarcely discernible. With the plants free from insects, if there is not satisfactory growth, one would be warranted in suspecting worms in the soil. I receive most speedy improvement by soaking

THE ROSE AS A HOUSE PLANT.

the soil, draining or skimming off any animal life that may arise, then applying a thin coating of finely pulverized soot. Again, I thrust the phosporous ends of a few matches in the pots, and saturating the soil with lime water is excellent, seeming also to give a beautiful verdure to the foliage. A few drops of carbolic acid solution added in watering plants is freely and successfully used by some, but it needs caution. It surely kills the worms, and may be used in severe cases upon old Roses without injury, but if any of the strong particles touch new or fleshy growth it is immediately blighted.

If you cannot shower your plants where they stand, remove them and shower them thoroughly as often as dry. The water from melted snow gives most thrifty results. Wipe off shelf and all surroundings with a damp cloth.

If, like myself, you reside in the bleak Northwest, you must provide against chills and severe draughts, especially upon buds. Let all soaking and showering be done with tepid water and when you can insure mild temperature. There must be fresh air, of temperature not often above 70° in the day time, cooler at night; but we, with our western winds, aud temperature that hovers too frequently around the minus forties, can only withdraw our treasures to a safe position, daring seldom to leave them near the glass at night.

If you wish to keep a large specimen, as a Marechal Neil, and weight is an objection, place it in a tin dish with ample surface and thorough drainage. Like the Fuchsia, the Rose delights in tin, and you can cover, paint tidily, or with good taste decorate, and the beauty of your plant will silence criticism. Later you may provide a box upon castors. Usually one will gain more satisfaction from a greater variety in smaller pots.

Roses incline to periodical blooming, with one longer season of rest each year. This longer season you may arrange at your pleasure, by denying free growth and blooming until you wish. Observing in the garden you will note that they send forth most rapidly the shoots bearing flower buds after a rainy season. When the buds are well towards blooming and for a space of time lasting until after the flowers are cut, I do not urge them, but afterwards shower and add fertilizers. You may fertilize very freely at any time when there is thrifty growth, for the Rose is a luxuriant consumer of food. If you desire speedy succession of bloom, you must place your plants every day the same side to the light, especially if you have only an ordinary window. Sometimes, when all has been done, a choice bud will refuse to expand. Keep all buds well washed, and you may assist by breathing into them, by carefully manipulating, or, if the calyx adhere, gently separate it.

The faint-hearted may count this care altogether too much trouble, yet a dozen Rose plants surrounded by most adverse circumstances, with active, intelligent care, will not require over an average time of five minutes each day; and if thus we can secure abundant bloom, how much more easily may it be done under favorable conditions.

As to the second division of my subject, individual taste has such variety that it is difficult to suggest. My own has so fully satisfied expectations that I incline to advise from it. Consult the descriptions of reliable Rose growers, comparing and choosing no novelties, unless you desire to experiment. You may rely upon the old, "profuse bloomers," Safrano, Bon Silene, Hermosa, Madame Margottin, Madame Rachel, etc.

Experience often differs in respect to varieties, for the reason, perhaps, that plants rooted from cuttings sometimes possess diverse tendencies; as one shoot from Perle des Jardins gives us the new Sunset, and, as one may often observe in a bush of two branches, where there is a constant recurrence of bloom upon one and little or none on the other. It is better not to expect as many flowers upon the choicer varieties as upon the old Sanguinea, though, possibly, some varieties may bloom as freely.

La France is sure of favor; Catharine Mermet and Perle des Jardins are beautiful in bloom, and their attractive foliage is a source of constant pleasure. The Marechal Neil secures to me its favor by its fragrance, which is unsurpassed.

A few of the most free blooming varieties in pots plunged in the open border will supply steady bloom from June until December, when they may be removed to the cellar. This season, an unusually trying one in the northwest, a Bourbon Queen, which bloomed freely the latter half of summer in a five-inch pot, gave no opportunity for removal except at expense of bud or blossom. La France, which bloomed sparingly late in the fall, was reset into a seven-inch pot, and it came into active growth and showed its flower buds the first of January. All buds, in this latitude, increase in size very slowly during December, but the approaching sun speeds them swiftly into bloom.

Read and study. The catalogues of florists are very valuable,

THE ROSE AS A HOUSE PLANT.

as you may readily discover if you give them consideration. All real flower lovers are generous of their knowledge and experience. Choose in accordance with your taste and surroundings, or, if you cannot decide, state them to the florist from whom you buy, and he will select wisely for you. Few pleasures are so cheaply bought as the enjoyment of these plants, which have been brought through all the tedious stages of their first growth.

If I were so unfortunate as to fail in blooming my Roses in winter, I should bed out my plants in the spring, layering branches for new growth, studying their habits more closely that I might provide more suitable conditions, meanwhile enjoying the flowers Dame Nature would be sure to bring.

I know no plant so sensitive to sympathetic treatment as the Rose, so quick to resent an injury, and yet so tenacious of life, even when reduced to the merest stalk, and so ready to forgive and send forth its blossoms with the first attentions. Intimate acquaintance will enable you to discern the drooping that indicates its poor health as readily as pallor in the face of a friend. How far will power may influence vegetation it may not be well to theorize, but I am sure that if you truly love Roses, you and your household may revel in their sweetness.

THE ROSE AS A HOUSE PLANT.

How can the Rose be managed as a house plant, and what varieties are most suitable for that purpose?

The only Roses that are likely to succeed when grown in the window garden, are a few varieties, and those belong to the Tea, Bourbon and Bengal classes. And to have them do well in the winter it will be necessary to commence preparations early in the spring, in order to have strong and healthy plants furnished with an abundance of healthy working roots, for the Rose is rather impatient when grown as a window plant; but a great deal will depend upon the treatment the plants receive.

Having procured the young plants early in the spring, they should be potted into three-inch pots, and placed in a warm and sunny situation. Water should be given when required and air on all favorable occasions. About the middle of May the plants should be repotted into four-inch pots and plunged to the rim of the pot in any sunny place in the open ground. After the plants are plunged they should be well mulched with coarse stable manure, and watered whenever necessary, and the very instant any flowers are noticed they should be removed. The pots should be turned at least once a week, in order to prevent the plants from rooting outside the pots to their manifest injury. This treatment should be continued up to the first of September, when the plants should be taken up and carefully examined, shifted into larger pots, if necessary, trimmed into shape, and placed in any sheltered situation until they are brought inside, which should be done before cold weather sets in, if they are intended for early blooming; while those intended for later bloom can be allowed to remain outside until the weather becomes cold, when they can be removed to a light, cool cellar, and afterwards be started into growth whenever it is deemed necessary to do so.

When brought inside they should be given a light, sunny place, windows having a southern exposure being preferred, and an average temperature of 50°. Water should be given as often as necessary, and two or three times a week liquid manure water. In watering, care must be taken not to render the ground cold and sodden, for water should never be permitted to remain around the roots for any length of time.

A GROUP OF TEA ROSES.

When grown inside, the Rose is very subject to the green fly and red spider, and I do not know of a more effectual remedy than Gishurst's compound applied according to the directions that accompany each box. This compound can be obtained at any seed store, and is the most effectual remedy in use for the window garden that I know of. Or the green fly can be destroyed by a slight fumigation of tobacco, and the red spider by freely syringing the plants with soapy water. In the window garden mildew is apt to be rather troublesome; this is caused by sudden changes in temperature as well as by damp, cloudy weather. For this, sulphur is an effectual remedy, and it can be applied by dipping the affected plant in water and then dusting it with sulphur.

The ensuing spring, as soon as the weather has become warm and settled, the plants should be turned out of their pots, and all the soil carefully removed from their roots. Then repot them in pots a size or two smaller, using fresh soil, and plunge and treat precisely as you did the year previously. About the first of September the plants should be taken up and repotted into pots of a larger size and trimmed into shape, the old wood and the long, scraggy branches being cut back to within five or six eyes of the main stems, then water thoroughly, place in a warm, sunny place, and bring inside before cold weather sets in. This treatment can be continued as long as the plants continue to grow strong and healthy, and when they cease to do this either plant them out in the flower border, or else throw them away and supply their places by those that are fresh and vigorous.

Roses require a rich, well mixed soil, the most suitable being composed of two-thirds well decayed sods from an old pasture, one-third well decayed stable manure with a fair sprinkling of bone dust; mix these materials thoroughly, and use the compost rough. In potting, use porous or soft baked pots, and let them be proportionate to the size of the plant. Be certain to drain the pots well, and in potting place the plant in the center of the pot, and water thoroughly to settle the plant.

The following varieties are the most suitable for window garden cultivation: Twelve Teas—Saffrano, Bon Silene, Isabella Sprunt, Rubens, Odorata, Perle des Jardins, General Tartas, Yellow Tea, Madame Bravy, Madame de Vatry, Madame Lambard and Souvenir d' un Ami. Four Bengals—Queen's Scarlet, Douglas, Duchess of Edinburgh and Ducher. Four Bourbons—Hermosa, Queen of Bourbons, Queen of Bedders and Edward de Desfosses. Besides these there is a class of recent introduction, known as the Polyantha Roses; they are of dwarf habit and are continually in bloom, the flowers being produced in clusters, and although the individual flowers are not large are very perfect. Of these, the most desirable are Mignonette, rose, Mlle. Cecile Brunner, salmon pink, Little White Pet, light pink, and Paquerette, pure white. Besides these we have the dwarf form of Rosa Indica, commonly called the Fairy Rose. It is a very pretty little miniature Rose, having double, rose-colored flowers, about the size of a dime. As it is constantly in bloom it is a plant that will always attract considerable attention, and is deserving of a place in every window garden.

THE STRAWBERRY.

To cultivate the Strawberry successfully for market it is first necessary, as in a logical argument, to establish correct premises, that is, to select a suitable location and soil, and to thoroughly fertilize and prepare the ground. In the selection of location, having first, of course, been satisfied that there is a remunerative market within reach, and that pickers can be readily obtained, get land, if you can, having both a northerly and southerly exposure, and soil suitable for the growth of the Strawberry. The best soil for the purpose is a deep, mellow loam which has sand enough in its composition to work freely; the next best is clay, if not too stiff, and with proper drainage facilities; the poorest is sandy land with a gravelly subsoil.

In obtaining a location with slopes, as recommended, try to have the soil of the portion sloping toward the south as warm and quick as possible, and while nature generally does much toward making vegetation on such slopes grow rapidly, assistance can be given by proper drainage, the use of such fertilizers as ashes and guano, and deep, thorough culture. The object of having land with different exposures and difference in quickness of soil is to prolong the Strawberry season. Upon the southern slope, early varieties can be grown and ripened from one week to ten days before the ordinary crop in the vicinity will be ready for market. By reversing the process, and using the northern slope for late varieties, the plants will bear fruit after the main crop is gone, and the owner of a plantation so situated will avoid a glutted market and realize better prices than less fortunate or less skillful competitors in the same line.

Land to be planted to Strawberries should have proper drainage, so that water does not stand upon or near the surface, yet the slope should not be so great that the land will wash. If there is not sufficient natural drainage, and in all cases, if possible, drain thoroughly with tile. The land should have been well cultivated with hoed crops for the two years next preceding Strawberry planting, in order to rid the soil of the white grub and to assist in killing out clover, blue grass and noxious weeds. Each year of such prior cultivation work into the soil all the stable manure that can be obtained; if that is not to be had, apply any fertilizer within reach, giving preference to those rich in potash, and put on all you can buy, beg or carry away.

In the fall after the second year's crop fertilize again, plow the ground deeply, if not underdrained, subsoil it and leave rough through the winter. In the spring following, as early as the ground is suitable to work, plow it again in a direction opposite to that traversed in the fall, using the subsoil plow in addition. After plowing, harrow thoroughly, making the soil fine.

The proper time to plant is as early in the spring as possible, especially if the plants are purchased. Plants from a distance will carry better and grow more surely in the cool, moist weather of the early spring time, when they are nearly dormant, than after a rank growth of vegetation has been made to heat and decay on the journey later in the season. I think it a good plan to order plants to arrive as soon as the frost is enough out of the ground to heel them in when received; then, upon arrival, to dig a shallow trench, laying the plants in singly, close, yet not crowding them, covering the roots with earth firmed carefully upon them. By so doing the plants are on hand when the ground is ready for them, they are fresh and keep so until favorable weather for planting allows them to be set. If you raise your own plants you can set them any favorable day, if you are careful, yet, as a rule, the earlier plants are set in the spring the better are the results.

The ground having been prepared, stretch lines at proper distances for the rows, have the plants ready, with roots straightened, and all dead leaves and runners removed; keep the stock of plants for each day in tubs, with water covering the roots, and make each person, while setting, keep his or her plants in a pail with a like root protection, not taking out a plant until ready to place it in the ground. Arm the planters each with a garden scoop or trowel; station them one at a row, and keep them always on the same side of the line until the rows are finished.

Set the plants thus: With a single blow drive the scoop into the ground to the depth of the blade and with the back of the blade toward the line; draw it forward enough to admit the plant's roots, thus leaving a straight side to the cavity next the line. Spread the roots of each plant in fan shape, and place them next to the straight side of the hole, then pack the earth firmly to the plant, covering all roots, yet leaving the crown exposed, and firm the plant in carefully. The important things to be observed are, keeping the plant roots wet while out of the ground, spreading them

THE STRAWBERRIES.

while setting, covering just right and carefully firming the earth around the plant. By making a direct stroke with the scoop and a straight side to the cavity for the plant the earth upon that side is left moist, and the roots being brought in contact with moisture grow readily even in a dry time.

I prefer using lines in setting, to any other method of marking the location of the rows; the plants set by line are upon a level with the surface, and not in a hollow to be covered with mud by the next rain, or upon a ridge to wither with succeeding drouth. Take pains in setting the plants; upon care in this, much of future success depends. Do not be anxious to hasten this work, remember that one plant that lives is worth a thousand that perish.

Growers of the Strawberry have several methods of culture from which to choose, and these methods may be classified and described as follows:

First, Hill Culture. By this system plants are set eighteen inches apart in the row, in rows three feet distant, and all runners are kept off as they appear, the plants forming crowns instead of young plants. Very large berries are grown in this way, and they are easily picked, but it is an uncertain method in sections where the winters are excessively cold and the snowfall light, as the plants suffer and frequently winter kill. Some varieties, as Jucunda, Sharpless and Bidwell seem particularly adapted to this method of culture on account of habits of growth. A modification of this method makes what is called the narrow row system, to grow thus: Set plants as in hill-culture, and instead of removing all runners allow one to remain and form a single plant in the row on each side of the parent plant, then remove all other runners from the new, and the old plants, as fast as they appear.

Second, the Matted Row. This method is most used by growers of Strawberries for market; by it plants are set from one to two feet apart in the row, and the rows are located from three and one-half to four feet apart, distances varying as the variety planted is feeble or vigorous in growth and in productiveness of plants. After setting, keep off the runners until the plants are well established, then let all grow. Keep the plants clean with hoe and cultivator until the young plants begin to take root, then suspend hoeing, but keep on cultivating as long as the season will permit, narrowing the cultivator as the plants spread, until at the end of the season the paths between the rows are about two feet in width. In cultivating always go the same way of the rows, that is, if you run next the row at the right in the beginning, keep next the row on that side at each succeeding cultivation. Have all weeds that appear in the rows after the runner plants begin to take root pulled out by hand, and let the persons removing the weeds at the same time straighten the runners and distribute the young plants forming, so that they will occupy the vacant spots, fixing them there with lumps of earth. The hand-weeding can be done by boys, very quickly and very cheaply, and is of great value to the plantation. The matted-row system can be modified to suit the wishes of the grower, so that the width of the rows or the number of plants will be increased or diminished.

A third system, sometimes adopted in the west, may be called the Matted Hill method. By this the ground is marked both ways, as for corn, three and one-half feet between the marks. Plants are set at the intersections, which are cultivated with a sulky corn-plow with guards on, until the runners are too numerous, then with a one horse cultivator to the end of season; all runners being allowed to grow and root. If the soil is not very weedy, fair crops of berries may be grown in this way without any hoeing.

In raising Strawberries by any method, have the rows twenty to twenty-five rods long, use horse-power as much as possible, keep clean, killing every weed as soon as it sprouts; keep the soil mellow, cultivating whenever the weather and the condition of the ground will permit. It has been said that "tillage is manure," and your berries will do better without manure than without tillage. By this method of cultivating, the surface will be kept level, and no ridges or furrows will be left between the rows.

In the fall, when freezing weather sets in, cover the plants two or three inches with wild hay, clean straw, sorghum bagasse, or any other coarse material that is free from weed seed, to prevent the plants from heaving.

In the spring, after the ground stops freezing, remove most of the covering into the paths between the rows, leaving enough around the plants to keep the berries clean, yet not so much as to retard growth, and let the covering placed in the paths remain to mulch the plants.

If there is prospect of a severe frost in blossoming time, get out all hands and work back a covering from the mulch in the paths, over the plants to shield them from the threatened danger. Unless early berries are desired, it is better to let the mulch remain upon the plants as long as possible in the spring, thus retarding blossoming and lessening danger from frost.

THE STRAWBERRY.

The great requisite of the Strawberry from the time it blooms until the berry matures is water; the mulch between the rows helps to keep the roots moist, but when the sun is like fire and the heavens as brass for about a week, the crop dwindles unless water is supplied. If you have no means of irrigation, try this plan: make a tank, water tight, the size of a wagon box, and a little deeper, sides and bottom of one and one-half inch boards. At the rear have a sprinkler attached, projecting one foot at each side beyond the wagon wheels; sprinkler of galvanized iron, four inches in diameter. Having beforehand arranged an elevated tank at the windmill, or a pump and platform in the pond, or some other water supply, off with the wagon box and on with the sprinkler, harness up, load with water, and from five in the afternoon until dark, and from daylight until seven in the morning wet down the plants driving astride the rows and watering three rows at a time. The expense of this method of watering is small, and there is no expenditure that will yield a more profitable return.

When the berry season arrives, keep close watch of the pickers; have them pick clean, don't let them pull the berries off, make them pinch off the stems. Do not allow unripe fruit, leaves or culls to go into the baskets, and do not allow the pickers to kneel on the plants, or skip any row, and discharge those who are careless or disorderly. Have a supply of tickets printed, most for one quart, next for four or six quarts, as the size of the pickers' trays may be; then, for such a number of quarts as will come to one dollar, or some other convenient multiple of the price per quart paid for picking, and give tickets for every quart of fruit as it is brought in.

Use clean, attractive packages; if for long shipment splint baskets are preferable, for a home market the veneer boxes answer very well. Always send good fruit to market, a little care in picking and handling will enhance values.

After the picking season is over, mow the plantation with a scythe, top-dress it liberally with well-rotted manure; with a twelve or fourteen inch stirring plow having a rolling coulter, throw two furrows together between the rows of plants, leaving the rows six or eight inches wide, then harrow thoroughly both ways, leave the plants until after a rain, and then hoe them out clean, and cultivate between the rows the rest of the season, letting all runners grow.

When the ground freezes, top-dress the rows with coarse manure, and the second crop will be nearly as good as the first.

After the second crop is picked, plow up the whole plantation and cultivate for two years before growing Strawberries on that plat of ground again.

*The selection of varieties depends upon the character of the market; if a large, high-flavored berry can be sold for a big price, grow Jucunda, Sharpless, Jersey Queen, and that class; if quantity is desired, plant Crescent, James Vick, Miner and Manchester; for a distant market you want firm berries, as the James Vick, Glendale and Wilson.

Pistillate varieties, like Crescent and Manchester, must be fertilized by planting with them staminate kinds that bloom at the same time, and I prefer the proportion of two rows of staminates to four rows of pistillates, to any other tried by me. Buy plants of reliable nurserymen, who will furnish what you order, of good quality and properly packed, and be willing to pay a fair price for what you buy.

And now, reader, having completed our journey together over the Strawberry fields, I must say, farewell, and may that "Providence that tempers the wind to the shorn lamb," favor you with gentle breezes and timely showers, that you may have Strawberries in abundance and wealth "galore;" such is my wish, for whatever counsel we take and experience we relate, yet much dependeth upon the weather.

---

*NOTE.—No fruit is more affected by the soil where it is raised than the Strawberry, consequently advice in regard to varieties must be considered as related to their general qualities. A few varieties only have been found adapted to large areas of territory and very varied conditions. Two varieties which have stood this test better than most others are the Wilson and the Crescent.

The suitableness of varieties for particular locations can be determined only by actual trial.—EDITOR.

THE RASPBERRY FOR MARKET.

Raspberries are among the most hardy and easily raised of small fruits. Land producing good crops of grain or roots will yield fair returns when planted with the Raspberry. Yet while this plant will endure imperfect soils and scanty culture much better than the Strawberry, the best results can only be had by thorough cultivation and high feeding. Raspberries consist of black, red and yellow varieties, and hereafter in this paper the word black will be used to designate one variety, and red for the other two, excepting when named. No small fruit does better with partial shade than the Black Caps. For the last six years we have had good crops from the Doolittle in an orchard set in 1865, trees six to ten inches through. We raise two rows of berries between the rows of trees, and the Apples are only twenty-six feet apart each way.

Plants of the black varieties are propagated from the tips of the canes; the best plants being produced from those bushes first set the preceeding spring; all plants showing disease or weak growth should be rejected. The red varieties are propagated from suckers, or, better still, from root cuttings in nursery rows, and should have their canes well ripened.

The black varieties should be set only in spring, and as early as the condition of the ground will allow. Plants for setting ought not to be taken up till about the time they are needed, and should be kept fresh, avoiding exposure to sun and wind. The red varieties may be safely set late in fall, and in many cases will do better if planted then. If they should be set in the spring they should be moved early. When plants can be had on the same farm, or in the same town, both kinds may be successfully planted later in the spring when the new growth has become four to six inches high; the method of transplanting being about like that for transplanting Tomatoes of that height. Setting green plants is often a convenience, although it involves more care, and is a much slower method.

The black varieties may be planted in rows seven feet apart and the plants two and one-half to three and one-half feet apart in the rows; and the red in rows six feet apart, with the plants from two and one-half to three and one-half feet apart in the rows. The red varieties are planted by eastern growers in rows running both ways, with the stools four to five feet apart. When planted three feet by six feet, two thousand four hundred and twenty plants are required to an acre; at three feet by six and one-half feet, two thousand two hundred and thirty-three plants, and at three feet by seven feet, two thousand and seventy-four plants.

The first year's cultivation consists in keeping the ground clean by the use of the cultivator and the hoe. In the fall, when the tips of the canes of the black varieties are ready, which can be told by their color and appearance, bury the ends two or three inches deep, going over the field twice for this purpose at an interval of a week or ten days. Late in the fall apply one-half of a large fork-full of manure to each space between the plants; both the black and red varieties should be treated in this manner. The manure serves as a mulch for winter protection of the roots, and is also an invaluable fertilizer as dissolved and washed down by rains and melting snow.

THE GREGG RASPBERRY.

The second year, as soon as the growth is two and one-half to three feet high, and not more, go through the field and pinch off the tips of all the canes. A week later go over again, nipping off all the tips overlooked, or those that were too small the first time. In the fall repeat the application of manure, as mentioned above. In the late fall remove all the old canes, but in places subject to deep snowfalls we advise letting the old canes of the black varieties remain till the following spring.

Picking and marketing are important operations. In cool weather pick once in three days, and when warm or rainy, each alternate day. Black Caps, if not allowed to get too ripe, will bear

THE RASPBERRY FOR MARKET. 55

shipping from fifty to one hundred and fifty miles. Most varieties of red Raspberries are not fit to ship more than fifty miles, and even

THE CUTHBERT RASPBERRY.

with the utmost caution losses in shipping red berries are almost unavoidable. The great bulk of the Raspberry crop is used by the canning factories. Two cents a quart is the standard price paid for picking, and boys and girls will average from twenty-five to fifty quarts in a day of ten hours' work.

Three varieties each, both of the red and black kinds, will be the least any grower for market should cultivate. Of the black, we advise the Souhegan for the first early, Tyler for second early, Doolittle and Ohio for medium, and Gregg for late; of red, Hansell for the first early, Turner for the second early, Philadelphia and Reliance medium, and Cuthbert late. All the above have been fully tested, and are entirely safe to plant. *I know of no variety of the yellow or orange Raspberry being grown here for field cultivation. Several years ago I tested Brinckle's Orange, but it was entirely too tender. Any variety raised by the acre must be hardy to be valuable.

The average crop of an acre of the Black Caps will range from fifteen hundred to three thousand quarts, and the average yield of the red varieties about the same. On our grounds a half acre planted on a piece fitted for a crop of Multiplier Onions, with the drills fifteen inches apart, and the Raspberry plants set in each fifth row, gave a first crop of about eight hundred quarts for the half acre; the second crop, of which an accurate account was kept, was, of berries marketed, a trifle over two thousand quarts, besides supply for family of six. The variety was the Doolittle. During this season, which was exceptionally cool and with frequent showers, fresh berries were picked for the table for four successive weeks. The season for marketing lasted three weeks. Last season, the price at the factory was eight cents a quart for Black Caps, and ten cents for red berries.

---

*The Golden Queen Raspberry is one of late introduction, but has now been well tested, and proves to be a fruit of great beauty, large size and great productiveness and high quaulity.

The Marlboro, a red variety appears to be specially valuable in certain locations, especially north. It is hardy and productive. Fruit large, bright crimson.—EDITOR.

THE BLACKBERRY.

Blackberry culture, like other kinds of business, requires a good comprehensive knowledge of its requirements, as well as thoroughness, in order to make it a success. If you do not understand the business fully you must learn it before you can succeed. Do not begin it on too large a scale, but begin moderately and work into it gradually, for you have to establish yourself in the business, not only as a producer, but as a marketer, and the latter, the disposing of a crop profitably, is full as important as the production of it. By commencing moderately, you avoid expense by raising instead of buying most of your plants, while you are at the same time building up a market for your products and advertising your business, which are both absolutely essential. The nearer markets are usually the best, and one can often sell direct to the consumer, and thus form a mutual and constantly increasing acquaintance, better than to depend entirely upon the distant commission houses, and the consequent largely increased competition which necessarily crowd in upon the large city markets, while at the same time, if your local market chances to be overstocked, you have the recourse to the other at any time for your surplus. Early fruit, as a general thing, pays best, and the next and even more essential requisite for success, is fine fruit, and put upon the market in the best and most attractive shape and condition. People will buy what suits their fancy in fruits as well as in other things, and the more attractive you can make its appearance the more salable and the better the price. Fine Apples, Peaches, Pears, Oranges, &c., are the fruits selected in the market, and you can make largely the same difference in the salability of smaller fruits.

Location, which gives ready access to market, climate and soil are the first requirements. It will probably not pay to try to raise Blackberries for market in a climate severe enough to require protection of the plants in winter, though you can select kinds which are more hardy than others and will succeed in a colder climate. The best soil is a good clay loam, comparatively new, or, at least, abundant in "humus," and well drained, and I think I can describe its requirements by saying such as will produce a fine crop of Potatoes. Old pasture or meadow land, well plowed in the fall, and, too, plowing in a pretty good growth of grass, instead of, as is frequently done, "pasturing it to death" before plowing, and the following spring planting it to Potatoes, with thorough cultivation of the growing crop, leaves the ground after digging the Potatoes in the fall, in the best possible condition for Blackberries; and I think I cannot too deeply impress the importance of a proper preparation of the soil before setting the plants. If you have not the sod or pasture land I have described, other good land will do. Plow it in the fall and sow to Rye, and then, in the following spring, when the Rye gets as tall as you can well cover, plow it under and harrow several times during summer, to keep down the weeds, without putting on any crop; then in the fall plow again and prepare thoroughly.

Don't go into the business from sudden fancy or impulse, but consider well what you propose to do, and plan particularly how you are going to do it before you begin. The fall is the best time to set the plants, as then they are ready for an early spring growth, and the roots will be growing and the plants becoming established before the frost is out, and the ground dry enough to work in the spring. If you have such ground, and in the condition I have described, it is preferable to land recently manured, and no manure need be applied until after the plants have borne, say two crops. In the absence of the clay loam I have recommended, the next best is good gravelly soil, and the least suitable a sandy one. Prepare the ground in the best manner to a good depth before setting the plants, and mix the soil well, so that it be in fine condition, and loose, and dry, and never undertake to set plants in the mud, or when the ground is in other than good condition.

The first plants must necessarily be bought, and buy only of good, reliable men, and get first class plants, true to name, and not mixed kinds, and be willing to pay a fair price for such. Good roots, well packed, are essential to success. The roots must be well protected, and in transportation and handling until finally set in the ground kept as much as possible from drying up. Have your ground all ready, except marking the rows, when your plants come, and then carefully heel them in near where you are to set them, covering the roots with fresh soil, so that if there is any delay in setting, the plants will not be suffering, and then you can take them out, a few at a time, keeping the roots shaded from the sunshine as much as possible while setting. Mark out your ground in furrows with a plow, in rows six or seven feet apart, and set the plants three and a half feet apart in the rows. If the kind set are moderate

THE BLACKBERRY.

growers, like the Wilsod's Early, make the rows six feet apart, and if they are rank growers, like the Lawton and Kittatinny, then seven feet apart.

I have found the most convenient way of distributing the plants in setting to be in a hand-cart, over which I put a cloth cover, somewhat similar to a covered wagon, and the cover raised high enough to permit the plants being handled beneath it, and thus kept in the shade until ready to be set, and if the weather is very drying they can be sprinkled thoroughly after being put in the cart for distribution. Then a good stout boy can run the cart along the rows and place the plants in position, while a man covers them with a hoe; set plants about the same depth that they grew, and make the hole large enough to allow the roots to be well straightened out, and tread the ground well around each plant with the feet. Do not spend time unnecessarily, but be sure that you bestow time and labor sufficient to make a good job of it, remembering that if any one is cheated by doing it carelessly, it always is yourself.

Each season, after setting, the ground must have thorough culture. Do not think that because the plants are for fruit they can take care of themselves, but give them as good clean culture as you do your Corn and Potatoes, beginning early in the season, but refraining from cultivation after September, to allow the plants to ripen up well before winter. When the plants are about three feet high, go through the rows and nip off the tops of the shoots in order to cause them to throw out lateral branches, and thus become self-supporting, and as the canes will be of different growth several nippings during the latter part of the season will be necessary, including also a shortening of the lateral branches when they begin to droop, making them much like miniature trees.

In each subsequent year, after the first, as soon as the plants have done bearing, cut out the old canes and remove them from the rows, as they will soon die any way, being of no further use, and if allowed to die on the plant, evidently hinder the growth of the new canes for the next year's bearing. Some claim that cutting them off and allowing them to remain till spring helps protect the plants during winter, and some recommend putting them between the rows and tramping them under foot; but I consider this a slovenly way of doing, and that it is better to remove them from the patch at once, and burn them.

If your ground is in such shape that you can do so, make long rows, so that in cultivating between the rows with a horse and cultivator you will be hindered less in turning. The plants will bear but little the first year, but the second year considerably, and the third year will come into full bearing, and if well cared for will be productive for ten years, provided, however, that the suckers are not allowed to grow too thickly, as all unnecessary canes must be mercilessly hoed up each year, in order to keep the rows in good condition, and the rows should be kept so as to mark the separate hills, and not allow them to form perfect hedge rows.

Blackberry sprouts are easily killed out when not wanted, or, if becoming too thick, by hoeing or cutting them during a dry time in summer, just at or below the surface, without digging, as that breaks the roots and causes them to sprout more freely. These suckers may be allowed to grow, and may be taken up in the fall to extend your patch, or set a new one whenever you need more plants, and it is better to save and use them instead of buying, unless you wish to try new kinds, as you can transplant them without having them so long out of the ground. You can also increase your stock by root cuttings, which make still better plants, though it takes them a year longer to come into bearing. Spade along one side of a row of vigorous growing plants and take up the outside roots in the fall, and cut them in pieces about three inches long, and bury them below the reach of frost until spring. Then they should be taken up as early as the weather will permit and planted two inches apart in nursery rows, about three inches below the surface and covered up about five inches deep, making a little ridge over the row, which should be raked off at Corn planting time, and if kept well cultivated will make strong plants for setting in the fall.

I have succeeded well, for some years past, with the Wilson's Early for early market, and Lawton and Kittatinny for late. Early fruit is the most profitable, the Wilson being marketed and all gone before the wild Blackberries ripen ! but in some seasons, when wild berries are plentiful, the late kinds bring a low price, but even then will pay, if by thorough cultivation you produce extra fine fruit.

Try new sorts sparingly until assured of their superiority and success. *The new kinds, such as Early Cluster, Stayman's Early,

---

*Of the more recently introduced varieties of Blackberries, the Early Harvest, Early King, Wilson Junior, Minnewaski, and the Erie have proved to be good and desirable sorts, and are all being planted for market as well as for private use.—EDITOR.

Stone's Hardy, etc., it is hoped will prove a valuable addition, but have not yet been tested sufficiently to determine with certainty but each grower should test them in a small way for himself, unless he finds them already a success in his own neighborhood. The Snyder Blackberry is very successful and bears a colder climate than most of the others.

In marketing your fruit, if a market is already established, it is well to ascertain and be guided by the most successful growers engaged in the business, and thus profit by their experience, without risk by experiment. I have found the thirty-quart crates, with me, the most salable, picking directly into the quart boxes without re-handling, as every time they are handled over the appearance and keeping qualities of the fruit are injured. Pick only fine fruit for market, and give good measure, liberal dealing being always the most successful, in other words, always do as you would like to be done by, and be sure your packages are neat and clean, and in appearance good. If you have had no experience in this, and have not the opportunity to see what are already a success in the market carefully look over advertising lists, and send to one or more reliable manufacturers for samples of berry boxes and crates, and then judge for yourself.

For the first year after your plants are set, you can profitably raise some rows of low-growing crops, such as Irish Potatoes, Sweet Potatoes or Beans between the rows, to help compensate for the necessary cultivation, but if that is done, it will be necessary to manure the soil after the first year, or your plants will suffer. I would most earnestly recommend, however, that every Blackberry grower also raise Strawberries and Raspberries. Then your Strawberries come into market first, and about a week after come the Raspberries, followed closely by the Blackberries, making it a continuous business during all the fore part of the season, and for the reason, too, that Strawberries can be planted in rows between the rows of Blackberries and help make the whole thing a success.

I have only one more recommendation to make, and that is a dry house or evaporator, and if a saving of expense is necessary, you can make a home-made one, which will answer a good purpose with little expense, in the shape of a small house with shallow drawers on the south side, and light slat bottoms, and so arranged that those nearest the fire can be exchanged and placed higher up when partly dried, and fresh berries put in their place, and heated by a stove underneath the drawers; in this way, if the market for your fruit gets too low for profit, you can evaporate the remainder of your crop, and thus market the dried fruit at a profit.

Before you undertake the growing of Blackberries, or, indeed, of any kind of fruit, become a subscriber to one or more reliable horticultural papers, and read them thoroughly; and also procure price lists from several good, reliable nurserymen, so you will be posted and not be at the mercy of traveling tree peddlers, who will be quite certain to visit you, asking enormous prices for stock often unreliable; and as long as you are interested in the business, keep yourself well posted, and in all things, if you expect success, try to deserve it.

APPLES.

The culture of the Apple is an important branch of farm and garden production. Not only is there a large home demand, but there is so good a foreign demand that it has come to be an important article of export. With the short crop the past season (1884) some sixty thousand barrels have been exported, seventy per cent. from New York, thirteen per cent. from Boston, and seventeen per cent. from Montreal. In 1882 some three hundred thousand barrels were exported. Apples are too high at home to be profitably exported this season. Liverpool is the great receiving port for American Apples. Besides those exported in the green state, many tons are exported in the form of canned or evaporated product. The evaporating and canning establishments greatly enhance the value of the poorer class of Apples, and prolong the season of Apples the year round.

Most all soils are good for Apple trees if thoroughly drained, either naturally or by good underdrains. On naturally heavy lands we would recommend setting the trees immediately over the drains, which should be laid at least three feet deep. The extending roots would be away, instead of toward the drain, and the tree itself would be in the best possible position for drainage. The ground between should be broken up deeply and thoroughly pulverized and manured. We are among those who believe in applying barn-yard manure, ground bone, ashes and compost liberally to all lands in Apple trees, and well working the fertilizers into the soil. We believe in mulching with any available material, even small stones or Spruce or Fir boughs, if nothing better is at hand, and a circle about the trunk of the tree whose circumference shall be beyond the outmost ends of the limbs. We believe in keeping the land among growing trees cultivated in some hoed crop, like Corn, Potatoes, Beans, roots, Peas or pickles, and in an annual manuring. After the trees have begun to bear well the land may be lightly stocked down to grass, and calves, sheep or swine pastured in the orchard to advantage. The mulching should be continued until the trees pretty much shade the ground. To prevent injury to the trees from the stock by oiling the trunks from the fleece or gnawing the bark with the teeth, drive a row of stakes inside a hogshead hoop or large cask hoop laid on the ground, with the tree in the center, then raise the hoop to the top of the stakes and nail each stake to the hoop. Brush piled up about the trunk is better than no protection. The animals keep down most of the grass and weeds and use up the wind-falls, immature and wormy fruit.

Much extent of trees may be grown along roadsides and permanent fences. The fence affords a partial mulch and trees do particularly well beside a stone wall. They are practically out of the way of the plow, harrow, mower, rake and other farm machinery. They may be set near together, one rod apart will do very well. On most farms enough orcharding may be had for all practical purposes by setting lines of trees by roadsides and permanent fences. It is not only practical, but adds beauty to the outlines and helps the landscape. There are also lots of natural orchard lands as yet unutilized, such as rough hillsides, nooks, corners, coves, gulches and rocky waste places. Nature, in fitting these natural sites for Apple trees, has spoiled them for most other purposes. Strong, vigorous volunteers on many of these attest the natural adaption. On these rough or waste lands trees may be set irregularly, and in most promising chances and places. They may be set thicker than on more arable lands. We believe that the best interests of our farmers and of our agriculture imperatively calls for the developing of these natural orchard lands.

If we were setting trees on good, arable land, we would set them in long rows, quite thickly in the row, with wide spaces between the rows, thus:

✳✳✳✳✳✳✳✳✳✳✳✳

✳✳✳✳✳✳✳✳✳✳✳✳

Why? Because this plan would admit of free cultivation or operation between the rows. It would admit of a continuous mulch along the rows, and admit free circulation air and sunlight, two important things, and of easy access to and among them with team. We would have them twelve to twenty feet apart in the row, and the rows to be four to six rods asunder.

Another plan is the "matted row," to borrow an expression from the Strawberry growers:

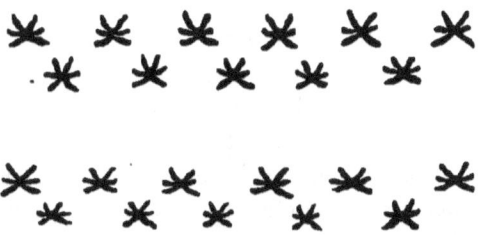

We should very much prefer one of these ways to either the square or quincunx form. It is very difficult to work among trees set in the usual way without injury to them from team or implements, or both.

Eternal vigilance is said to be the price of fruit. The caterpillar, canker worm, fall web-worm, borer, codlin moth head the list of many formidable insect enemies. The bark louse, and Apple maggot, Trypeta pomanella, a new comer, by the way, that burrows and permeates the pulp in all directions, itself, when grown, hardly the sixteenth of an inch long, are to be met and fought. The whale oil soap, and knife and wire, and many other appliances are needed in the fight for fruit. The novice must study his business, and the experienced have need to practice all they know. But what branch of farm production is exempt from insect enemies or climatic conditions?

The key of the whole position is fertilization. Feed the trees and they will pay you. The better trees are fed and cared for the faster they grow and the sooner they bear. The faster they are pushed the sooner the investment pays; the less time the caterpillar and the borer has to work upon them. As a rule, the orchards are not half fed. The Apples of the United States might be improved as a whole one hundred per cent., both in quality and amount from the present bearing trees by manuring alone. This is a fact that cannot be gone behind successfully. We believe in working an orchard or a fruit tree for all it is worth, for all it has capacity.

Near cities and ready markets the best summer and fall varieties will pay well; but for the great bulk of the crop of the country it is wisdom to grow those best hardy varieties that are hard in flesh, long keepers, and at the same time well colored and pleasing to the eye. Quality is to be sought for, and our best winter and spring

Apples will give, on the whole, the most satisfactory returns. In planting a new orchard be careful to select varieties best adapted to the particular locality, and this information should be gained from the most trustworthy sources. Raise only fine varieties. Pack them honestly. Carefully hand-pick them from the tree. Keep them, until sold, in a moderately damp cellar, but a few degrees above the freezing point. Have the cellar fairly ventilated. Wash out and dry each barrel before putting Apples in for the market. Reputation for good, honest Apples once established and followed up, means sometimes one dollar a barrel over questionable lots. "Honesty is the best policy," said the old man to his son, "I have tried both." Set none but first-class trees; set good sized trees; set them carefully. Use plenty bone and ashes about them. Study the varieties best adapted to the locality. Feed liberally, care for them sensibly, and success will crown the work.

GRAPE-VINES.

Planting and management of Grape-vines in the family garden.

For Eastern, Middle or Western States success in Grape culture, either in the field or garden, will depend upon the following points: 1st, Soil and location; 2d, Preparation of the ground and planting; 3d, Pruning and training; 4th, Winter protection; 5th, Varieties.

1st, Soil and location. As it regards chemical composition, the Grape succeeds on a wide range. Thin, rocky slate, deep porous gravel, hard tenacious clay, all, though not equally well, bear fairly good crops. The gravel usually excels in quantity, the slate and clay in quality. In one respect the vine is exacting. The soil must be dry and well drained. The location should be sunny, warm and airy. Localities having a breeze from off bodies of water are good. Warm hillsides, when terraced, are admirable. If near buildings, choose the south or east sides, but do not train on to a building, but to a trellis a few feet off, as there is a better circulation of air.

2d. Preparation of the ground and planting. Most garden soils are rich enough for vines. Plant in the spring, and plant deep. Make a broad open place, not less than fifteen inches deep, and in porous soils go down from twenty to twenty-two inches. Cover the roots with surface soil, not letting any fresh manure come in contact, and do not, at first, fill the hole for the vine over half full. Select vines as graded first-class one year, or first-class two years, and, if possible, choose only those having many fibrous roots. Before planting cut back the roots to twelve or fifteen inches, and the top to six inches. After six or eight inches of soil has been put on the roots, a covering of unrotted manure will serve as a mulch and later as a fertilizer. Broken bones are excellent put near the roots in planting, and after the vine is old enough to bear pour around the roots the soap suds from the kitchen. Avoid an excess of animal manures, using ashes, leached and unleached, bone dust or mineral fertilizers.

3d. Pruning and training. To attempt to grow Grapes, even in the garden, without learning enough of the habit of the vine to give some form of pruning, is simply folly. If in the most favored regions on the most natural Grape soil, vines untrimmed speedily come to disease and ruin, how much more will this be true where success is less easily secured. The limits of this article will not allow a full description of methods of pruning, but I shall present a few elementary principles. The fruit of any one season comes from buds on the canes of the previous year's growth. This growth of last season is the new wood, and all former growth is known as the old wood. New wood is known by its smooth, firm bark, the bark on all old wood being scaly or loose on the outer part. Vines eight feet apart each way are pruned so as to leave not more than five nor less than two canes of new wood for bearing, each cane two and one-half to three feet long. The first two seasons are given to growing new wood only, the first crop of fruit being borne the third season, and the foregoing is applicable to the seasons following the third. Two canes are enough for the first crop of fruit. As to methods of training, we give several, taking the simplest first.

a. Stakes. Each vine requires two stakes set two feet apart, the vine midway between, the stakes five feet above ground, and two feet or more deep, so as to be perfeetly firm, the canes being firmly tacked to the stakes, crossing from one to the other.

b. Post and trellis. This method of training is to be preferred to stakes. Plant the vines eight feet apart in a perfectly straight line. When only two vines are grown, a good plan is as follows: Set a post seven feet long and two and one-half feet deep; two feet from this plant a vine, four feet from the vine set another post, four feet from this another vine, two feet from this the third post. To the posts firmly nail three slats, each sixteen feet long by four inches wide, putting one slat at the top of the posts, one eighteen inches from the ground and the third between the others. When three or more vines are planted in each row use wire No. 9 or 10, instead of slats, firmly bracing the end posts, and if the posts are set firmly they will do if only set between each alternate vine. A very simple summer house may be made by setting posts at each angle of an octagon, each side of which is eight feet, and plant the vines midway between the posts. Vines should never be trained immediately upon the side of a dwelling house or other building, but upon a trellis standing four to six feet from it. The fruit will be much better and the vine can be far more easily managed. Vines can easily be trained to form an admirable screen, which, with proper annual pruning, will be for a life-time a thing of beauty and a source of profit.

4th. Winter protection. All tender varieties, such as Rogers' hybrids and many others, should have, after the leaves have fallen, the canes taken off the trellis and laid upon the ground, covering from one to three inches with soil. This affords a perfectly simple, safe and sure protection, and must not be omitted. Uncover in the spring after the ground will do to work, and not before.

5th. Varieties. For first early, select Moore's Early and Hartford; the Tallman or Champion is of too poor quality. For second early, plant Concord, Worden, Wilder (Rogers' No. 4), Telegraph of the black sorts; Brighton, Lindley (Rogers' No. 9), and Delaware of the red Grapes; Martha, and your choice from Dutchess, Pocklington, *Prentiss, of the white varieties. Very nearly all these are strictly hardy Grapes, and all have an established reputation. There are several non-enumerated later Grapes, but for the garden we advise to try the first earliest sorts. If these succeed in all seasons it is easy to add to the list.

---

*NOTE.—Since the above was written, further trial has shown that the Prentiss is not a variety that can be relied upon for general cultivation—it, perhaps, may do well in some localities and with special treatment, but it is apparently lacking in vigor, and its foliage is not very resistant to mildew.

The Jessica is an excellent, very early, greenish Grape suitable for the garden, and the Diamond, which ripens a little later and about the time of the Delaware, is the handsomest and best of all the white varieties. The Winchell is a very promising white variety, suitable for the garden.— EDITOR.

MUSHROOM GROWING.

It has often been a matter of surprise to me that the Mushroom is not raised more generally and extensively in this country than it is. I know there are a few places where it is grown for market, and made very profitable, but these places are not one-twentieth part as numerous as they ought to be. I know of no good reason why the Mushroom should not be grown in large quantities and with a large profit on the capital invested, in the vicinity of any large town or city. I think that the main reason why it is not cultivated more extensively is that most people have an idea that there are certain mysterious and intricate processes to be gone through which are too deep and difficult for the comprehension of common mortals; now, the sooner this idea is dispelled, the better for all concerned. And I will here make the assertion that there is no more difficulty in growing Mushrooms in large quantities, for market, than there is in growing Potatoes, or any other vegetables, that is, if the directions I am about to give are adhered to.

Mushroom growing on a large scale cannot very well be carried on at a long distance from a large town or city, because fresh horse manure, which is one of the principal materials, can only be had in quantity where a large number of horses are kept. The most suitable place, if the rent is not too high, would be a cellar or basement under a public hall, or manufacturing establishment; if this cannot be had, any building where a temperature of from $45°$ to $60°$ can be maintained during winter will answer the purpose. I am supposing that the person who is about to start intends to make a business of it, so I will give directions for fitting up the space in a permanent manner. The most convenient width for the beds, when there is a walk on each side, is six feet, and as long as the house will allow; a building thirty feet wide would give room for three beds, each six feet wide, with a walk three feet wide between and around them; and to economize space, two beds may be made, one above the other, arranged in the following manner: take good, sound, three by four scantling, in lengths to reach from the floor to the joists; nail these upright, in straight rows, six feet apart, and four feet between the uprights in the rows; next, take pine boards, one inch thick, place these edgewise on the floor, and nail to the uprights; this gives a bed six feet wide and twelve inches deep on the floor; next, take good, sound boards one inch thick, and six feet long, and nail these edgewise on the uprights, with the upper edges four feet from the floor; on these lay one inch boards close together, to form a floor for the upper bed, and nail these boards down to the cross pieces. Then take boards twelve inches wide and one inch thick, and nail them edgewise to the upright, to form sides for the upper beds, and then you will have your beds ready for the material in which the Mushrooms are to be grown.

AGARICUS CAMPESTRIS.

The material to fill in the beds is from droppings; take fresh horse droppings from the stables, in as large a quantity as can be procured, to which add an equal weight of fresh loam from a pasture field; old soil that has been worked or manured must not, on any account, be used. Let the loam and droppings be well mixed together from day to day as they are received, or, if enough can be procured at one time, all the better. Place the heap in some outbuilding, where it cannot get the least wet. If it is not all procured at once, turn the heap over every day, to prevent too violent heating, until enough is on hand to fill the bed, or beds. Now, all is ready for filling the beds, which should be done as follows: take from the heap of manure and soil prepared as above directed, enough to form a thin layer over the bottom of the bed or beds; pound this down quite firmly with a mallet or square block of wood, then another layer beaten down like the first, and this must be repeated until you have a depth of eight inches, neither more nor less; if it is deeper than eight inches, it sometimes reaches too high a degree of fermentation, but less than eight inches is not quite enough. Having done this, plunge a thermometer into the bed, which, in about two days, will heat enough to run the mercury up to more than 100° Fahrenheit; wait until this goes down to about 90°, then take a sharp stick and make holes in the bed about a foot apart each way, and about half as deep as the bed; into each of these holes put a piece of spawn about an inch and a half square, cover the holes up again so that the surface of the bed will be level and firm as it was before the spawn was put in.

Nothing is now to be done for about twelve days, when the spawn will have "run" through the whole bed. Next, spread over the whole surface of the bed a layer two inches thick of fine, fresh loam, pressed down moderately firm and quite level, cover the bed with about four inches of nice, clean hay or straw; now there is nothing to do but to keep a proper degree of heat, which should be as near 60° as possible all the time; but it must on no account be allowed to go below 45° at any time, or else the beds will get cold too soon, and the crop be too late to be profitable. If the air of the house or cellar is not very dry, no water will be required; but the beds must be examined occasionally, and if the surface is dry, give a light watering from a fine rose watering-pot, with the water heated to about 100°.

With the above treatment commencing in November, the first crop will be ready in January. The Mushrooms don't all come up at once, so the gathering of the crop will last about three weeks. After the first crop is all gathered, spread about half an inch of fresh loam over the bed, beat down firm and level, and gently water with warm water when it becomes dry, and cover up as before, with hay or straw, and another crop, frequently better than the first, will be gathered in February. Mushroom spawn of good quality can be obtained from any good seedsman. It is imported frequently in order to be fresh.

*GROWING MUSHROOMS.

Mr. John G. Gardner, of Jobstown, (about a dozen miles from Trenton, N. J., I should think), grows Mushrooms largely and successfully, and all for market. It isn't a matter of experiment and fancy with him at all, but one of profit—his bread and butter depend upon it. He grows them in frames inside his cool greenhouses, also in a large, frost-proof cellar under a hay barn. Now this cellar is simply an ordinary cellar, such as any farmer in the country has, and the little that has been done to it to darken the windows and make them tight so as to render them better for Mushrooms, any farmer with a hand-saw, an axe, a hammer and a few nails and some boards can do. Mr. Gardner is a market gardener and has not the amount of fresh manure upon his own place that he needs for Mushroom growing, but he buys it in New York and thence gets it shipped to him by rail. And this pays. Now, if it will pay a man to get manure at such a cost for Mushroom growing, how much more will Mushroom growing pay the farmer who has the cellar and the manure as well? Mr. Gardner raises Mushrooms and lots of them, and any one who is interested in this direction can go right to see for himself. I was there on November 28th, and saw them, a capital crop, and Mr. Gardner, instead of trying to hide anything in their cultivation from me, took particular pains to show and explain everything about his way of growing them. He assures me that by the old complicated and troublesome way of preparing the manure and "fixing" for the crop, he couldn't make any money by growing Mushrooms, but by the simple means he now practices he gets good crops, good Mushrooms, good prices and good profits. As the cellar method is the most available one for farmers, this is the one I will describe in detail :

The cellar is sixty feet long, twenty-four feet wide and nine feet high from floor to ceiling. The floor is an earthen one, but perfetly dry. It is well supplied with window ventilators and doors, and in the ceiling, in the middle of the cellar, opens a tall shaft or chimney-like ventilator that passes straight up through the roof above. While the beds are being made full ventilaton by doors,

---

*Note.—This article was contributed to the Rural New Yorker in 1888.

windows and shaft is given, but as soon as there is any sign of the Mushrooms appearing all ventilators, except the shaft in the middle, are shut up closely and thenceforward kept shut.

The manure used in forming the beds is common horse stable manure and is brought here from Jersey City, over seventy miles on railroad cars.

The soil used for mixing with the manure and for surfacing the beds is ordinary vegetable-garden loam.

The bed occupies the whole surface of the cellar floor and was all made up on one day. As a pathway a single row of boards is laid on the top of the bed, running lengthwise along the middle of the cellar from the door to the farther end, and here and there between this narrow path and the walls on either side, a few pieces of slate are laid down on the bed to step on when gathering the Mushrooms.

Making the bed. Now here comes the oddest thing about MR. GARDNER's Mushroom-growing. He doesn't prepare the manure in any way whatever for the Mushroom beds. He hauls it right from the cars to the cellar and at once spreads it upon the floor and packs it solid into a bed. For the bed now in bearing the manure arrived at Jobstown on September 8th, and it was hauled home and the bed made up the same day, and the first Mushrooms were gathered from this bed the second week in November, just in two months from the time the manure left the Jersey City or New York city stables. The bed is fifteen inches thick. In making it the manure was first shaken up loosely to admit of its being more evenly spread than if pitched out in heavy forkfuls, and it was then tramped down firmly with the feet. The bed was then marked off into halves. On one half (No. 1) a little over a three inch deep layer of loam was at once laid over the manure; on the other half (No. 2) no loam was put on at this time, but the manure on the surface of the bed—about three inches deep—was forked over loosely. Twelve days after having been put in, the temperature of the bed No. 2, three inches deep, was 90°, and then it was spawned on the 28th. Next day the soil from bed No. 1 was thrown over on to bed No. 2, which was spawned on the 24th, and then part of the soil that was thrown on No. 1 was thrown back again on No. 2, so that now a coating of loam one and a half inches deep covered the whole surface of the bed. When finished, the surface was tamped gently with a tamper whose face is a piece of pine plank sixteen inches long by twelve inches wide. Mr. G. does not believe in the alleged advantages of a hard packed surface on the Mushroom bed, but is inclined to favor a moderately firm one.

Spawn. He uses the English brick spawn which is sold by all of our seedsmen. He has tried making his own spawn, but owing to not having proper means of trying it, he has met with indifferent success.

Spawning the beds. Almost all Mushroom growers insert the pieces of spawn about two or three inches under the surface of the manure, one piece at a time, aud at regular intervals of eight or nine inches apart each way—lengthwise and crosswise. But here again Mr. G. displays his individuality. He breaks up the spawn in the usual way, in pieces one or two inches square. Of course, in breaking it up there is a good deal of fine stuff besides the lumps. And now with a diamond-pointed hoe he draws drills eighteen inches apart and two and a half to three inches deep lengthwise along the bed, and in the rows he sows the spawn as if he were sowing Peach stones or Walnuts or Snap Beans, and cover it in as if it were seeds.

Air and temperature. Mr. G. regards 57° as the most suitable for Mushroom growing, and if possible, he maintains this without the aid of fire-heat. He has hot-water pipes connected with the contiguous greenhouse heating arrangement in his cellar, but he never uses them for heating the Mushroom cellar except when obliged to. By mulching his bed with straw he could get along without any fire-heat, but then this wonld be very awkward when gathering the Mushrooms.

Top dressing. After the bed has borne a little while, Mr. G. assured me he finds that top dressing it all over with a half inch deep layer of fine soil is very beneficial to it. Before using, this soil had been kept in a close place—pit, frame, shed, or large box —in which there was at the same time a lot of steaming-hot manure so that it might become thoroughly charged with Mushroom food absorbed from the steam from the fermenting material.

Watering. Should any portion of the bed get very dry, water it gently and somewhat sparingly, with water at a temperature of about 90° through a fine-rosed water-pot or syringe. Never give enough water at a time to penetrate to the manure and the spawn below the coating of earth. But rather than make a practice of watering the beds Mr. G. finds it is much better to maintain a moist atmosphere by—when needed—sprinkling the walls and ceiling with tepid water from a syringe.

Food and moisture. And here is an idea of MR. GARDNER'S own, which I never before saw in practice in the same way. He firmly believes that the Mushrooms derive much nourishment from the "steam" of fermenting fresh horse manure, and by using this "steam" in our Mushroom houses we can maintain an atmosphere almost moist enough to be able to dispense with the use of the syringe, and the Mushrooms are fatter and heavier for it. And he practices what he preaches. In one end of his Mushroom house he has a very large, deep, open box half filled with steaming-hot horse droppings, and once or twice a day he tosses these over with a dung fork in order to raise a "steam," which it certainly does. It is also for this purpose that he introduces the loam so soon when making the beds, so that it may become charged with food that would otherwise become dissipated in the atmosphere.

Varieties of Mushrooms. Of course there is a marked difference between the Mushrooms raised from the French flake spawn and those from the English brick spawn; but he has never observed any distinct varieties from the same kind of spawn. Sometimes a few Mushrooms will appear that are somewhat differently formed from those of the general crop, but this he regards as the result of cultural conditions rather than of true varietal differences.

The duration of a bed. His bed began bearing early in November and he expects it will continue to bear a good crop till the first of May next; after that time no matter what the crop may be, the Mushrooms become so infested with maggots as to be perfectly worthless and they may at once be cleared out. It is on account of the large body of manure in the bed and the low, genial and equable temperature of the cellar that the beds in this house always continue so long in good cropping condition.

Gathering and marketing. Some years ago the Mushrooms were not gathered till their heads had opened out flat, but nowadays the market men don't want them that way; they like to get them when they are quite young and before the frill between the cap and stem has broken apart. A good market is found in Philadelphia, New York and Boston. The Mushrooms are shipped by express in twelve pound baskets. A layer two deep is laid in the bottom of the basket, then some paper, then another layer. All Mushrooms whose caps are broken are rejected, and those whose frill has burst are laid on the top layer. Baskets are far more carefully handled by expressmen than are boxes and they cost very little. The supply has never been nearly equal to the demand.

ASPARAGUS.

The first thing to be done by one who wishes to grow Asparagus for market, is to see if he has any soil that is suitable. It should be a light loam and as deep as it is possible to obtain. Asparagus will grow on almost any soil, but I do not think that its cultivation will prove profitable on a heavy clay soil, nor where a stiff clay subsoil comes up within a few inches of the surface. It can be made profitable on very light sand by the use of plenty of manure.

The next thing is to arrange for a supply of plants. These can either be pnrchased from some nurseryman, or can be grown from the seed on one's own land. Dry Asparagus seed when sown in the open ground, is very slow to germinate, and it is difficult to prevent the weeds from taking possession of the ground before the Asparagus plants appear. My own plan has been to soak the seed in hot water until swollen and softened before sowing. It should be sown in long rows a foot or more apart, so as to be tended with a hand or horse cultivator. If a few Radish or Cabbage seeds are sown with the Asparagus they will come up at once and show where the rows are, so that they can be cultivated before the Asparagus appears. Some growers, after soaking the seed, put it into a coarse bag and bury it deep in the ground until it begins to sprout, and then when sown it comes up immediately. Whichever plan you adopt, be sure and keep the plants clear of weeds through the season. As you are growing the plants for your own use, you will want them to be as large and strong as possible, therefore sow plenty of seed, and then when weeding them, thin out the plants to about three inches apart. To make good plants the soil mnst be very rich, so do not be stingy with your manure.

During the season, while your plants are growing, you should prepare the permanent bed. It is not necessary, as was formerly supposed, to dig out all the earth to the depth of two or three feet and then fill in the bottom with all manner of trash and fertilizing material, such as old boots, bones, etc. The land must be deeply plowed and thoroughly pulverized. It cannot be made too rich; with the possible exception of Rhubarb, Asparagus is the most gross feeder of any vegetable in cultivation. A successful market gardener in Illinois, writing some years ago, upon the raising of Asparagus for market, used the following language: " The profits are just in proportion to the amount of manure used, which should be more than most people think enough." This is strictly true. He also said, "Study economy in the processes of labor, using the horse instead of the hand, and the rake instead of the fingers, whenever possible, but be unsparing of manure." No better advice than this could possibly be given, and the grower may expect that his success will be exactly in proportion to the fidelity with which he follows these directions. The kind of manure and its mechanical condition when applied to an old bed are not material. Fresh stable manure may be used, no matter how coarse so long as it can be plowed under. But in preparing the ground for a new bed fine, well rotted manure is to be preferred. Asparagus always starts into growth very early in the season, and the bed should be plowed late in the fall that it may dry out and be ready to work as early as possible in the spring.

The proper distance between the rows and between the plants in the rows is a matter of dispute. Years ago the rule was three feet between the rows, and from twelve to eighteen inches between the plants. This is universally conceded now to be too close, two by three or four feet, usually the last, is the closest planting allowed. Many set their plants four feet apart each way and cultivate the bed both ways. The growers of the celebrated Oyster Bay Asparagus make their rows five or six feet apart and set the plants two or more feet apart in the rows. In planting, the crowns should be set at least three inches under ground, and in many places four or five inches would be better.

The first season all that is necessary is to keep the bed clear of weeds and the surface mellow. In most parts of the north winter protection is a great benefit. If there is no danger of injury to the plants from severe cold still a heavy mulch, put on before the ground freezes, will keep all, or nearly all, the frost out of the soil, so that the bed will start very much earlier in the spring. A thick coating of fresh stable manure is the best possible mulch, and that is also an excellent way to apply manure. The coarsest of the litter should be raked off in the spring and the balance plowed under. This may be supplemented by the application of a few hundred pounds per acre of some good commercial fertilizer. Ground bone is one of the best.

The question, whether salt is needed on an Asparagus bed, is by no means settled. While some claim that it is necessary and should be applied every year, others say that Asparagus does not need salt any more than any other vegetable. Without undertaking to decide the question, it is certain that Asparagus is not injured by the application of sufficient salt to destroy almost all other vegetation near it. If not specially useful as a fertilizer, the free use of salt on an Asparagus bed is an advantage; it has a tendency to prevent the growth of weeds, and by attracting moisture from the atmosphere helps to carry the bed safely through a drouth. Coarse or refuse salt may be applied every spring, and enough can be used to make the surface of the soil look quite white. Old brine from pork or beef barrels may often be obtained without expense from butchers, but care should be used in applying it, for it is possible to kill Asparagus roots with brine, as I know from personal experience.

In the spring run a cultivator along the top of each row two or three times and then harrow, that the soil over the plants may be very loose. Between the rows stir the soil often enough to keep it mellow and clear of weeds until the tops shade the ground. The second year a little Asparagus may be cut, but be very careful not to continue the cutting too long. The third year a little more may be used, but a full crop cannot be expected until the fourth year. It is a good plan each year, when you stop cutting, to apply at that time a liberal dressing of stable manure or fertilizer and cultivate it in; the object of this is to insure a strong growth of tops and roots during the summer and fall, for the amount of the next crop depends upon the growth made this fall. In autumn, just before the seed balls are ripe enough to drop off easily, mow all the tops, haul them away and burn them; otherwise the ripe seed falling upon the bed will grow there, and young Asparagus plants are very undesirable weeds anywhere and especially so in an Asparagus bed.

Oyster Bay Asparagus is very popular in New York city; it is all white, being cut eight or ten inches under ground as soon as the top shows itself above the surface. They make their rows five or six feet apart and set the crowns very deep under ground. Every spring they plow up the earth between the rows until it is very mellow, and then with plows and other tools specially contrived for the purpose, they ridge up the earth over the rows until the bed looks very much as if it were intended for plantiug Sweet Potatoes, except that the ridges are broader and are not sharp but rounded off rather flat. Though this blanched Asparagus sells for a higher price in New York city, yet as it costs much more in time and labor to grow and gather it, I doubt if it would generally prove any more profitable than that grown in the ordinary way.

Asparagus should always be cut a little below the surface of the ground, if for no other reason than that the sharp stubs left may be out of the way. Asparagus knives are advertised which are quite broad and are sharpened across the end, and are intended to cut by shoving straight down against the stalks; but this form and all common knives become dull so soon that it is necessary to carry a whetstone constantly, and to use it every few minutes. Some of the large growers on Long Island use a common heavy knife having a few teeth, like saw teeth, filed into the edge near the the point. Such a knife can be used for half a day without becoming too dull.

The stalks must always be cut before the heads show any signs of breaking or branching out; the lengths should range from six to ten inches. The size of the bunches must depend upon the market in which it is to be sold; for New York city they should be four or five inches in diameter, about seven or eight inches in length, and should weigh from three to three and one-half pounds. To put up such large bunches in good shape requires the use of a bunching machine, which costs from three to four dollars. In western markets the size varies according to the taste of the growers. For Chicago market a good salable size is about three inches in diameter and from six to nine inches in length. Great pains should be taken to have the tops exactly even, and after the bunch is tied up the bottom should be cut off square, so that all the stalks will be exactly the same length. The bunches should be tied in two places, near the top and near the bottom. The tying material must be broad and soft, common twine will not do, as it cuts into the stalks too much. I have seen it tied with strips of white cotton cloth, having the name of the grower printed upon them, so that every bunch sold advertised his business. Bass bark is one of the best tying materials, and is probably most commonly used.

If the crop is to be shipped to a distant market it is packed in crates with tight bottoms, but with slat sides and tops. The crate should be large enough to hold three or four dozen bunches, and just deep enough for one layer of bunches when standing upright. The Asparagus should be perfectly dry when put into the crate; this is indispensible, otherwise it will surely heat and spoil, and it should be packed so snugly as to prevent shaking about in the crate, which would perhaps cause the tender tops to be broken off,

ASPARAGUS.

thus rendering the Asparagus unsalable. Shippers from Charleston and other Southern ports often put a layer of perfectly dry moss over the bunches to protect the tops. When shipped a long distance, a layer of wet sand or moss in the bottom of the crate, on which to set the bunches, will help to keep them from wilting.

The profits of growing Asparagus depends so much on soil manure, cultivation and market that it is difficult to fix on any reasonable average. The range is all way from $100 to $1000 per acre; the average is probably much nearer the first figure than the last. Usually, however, that is the fault of the grower. If he is stingy of manure and cultivation, he illustrates the old adage, "He saves at the spigot and wastes at the bung-hole."

PEAS.

What varieties of Peas are most profitable for the market gardener, and what most desirable for the table, and what are best methods of cultivation in each case?

The Pea is a vegetable that can only be grown to the greatest perfection in a comparatively low temperature, and therefore it should be planted as early in the spring as the ground can be worked.

The best and most profitable kinds for early market, I have found to be Blue Peter, Carter's First Crop, Bliss' American Wonder, Little Gem and Improved Daniel O'Rourke.

To grow these varieties to the greatest perfection a warm, sunny soil is most suitable; it must be thoroughly enriched with well-rotted manure, or bone dust applied at the rate of fifteen hundred pounds to the acre and well harrowed in. The next operation is marking out the rows, which for Carter's First Crop and Improved Daniel O'Rourke should be three inches deep and thirty inches apart. For Blue Peter, Little Gem and Bliss' American Wonder, the rows may be twenty-four inches apart. As soon as the Peas are out of the ground about two inches, hoe or cultivate between the rows, and repeat the operation at intervals of ten days for about four weeks, when a little soil may be drawn up to the rows on each side. This is all the working they require before gathering the crop. No sticks or brush need be used. Again, I would endeavor to impress the grower with the importance of sowing just as soon as the ground can be worked, as the first Peas in the market fetch by far the highest prices. About two and one-half bushels will sow an acre.

Varieties of Peas for a family to grow for table, and mode of cultivation:

The best kinds of Peas for use for a private family are Blue Peter, Waite's Caractacus and Laxton's Alpha for first crop; McLean's Advancer and Laxton's Prolific Long Pod for second early, and Champion of England and Telephone for later crop.

The ground should be dug deep and well manured with thoroughly rotted manure, or bone dust spread on the surface, one pound to the square yard and well raked in. Sow in double rows about eight inches apart and four inches deep, and leave a space of about thirty inches between each double row. A quart of early varieties will sow about seventy feet of drill, of the later kinds about fifty feet.

To keep up a succession, sow as follows: April 1st, one quart of Blue Peter; April 10th, one quart of Waite's Caractacus; April 20th, one quart of Laxton's Alpha; April 30th, one quart McLean's Advancer; May 10th, one quart Laxton's Prolific Long Pod; May 20th, one quart Champion of England; May 30th, one quart Telephone. After this date none may be sown until about the middle of August, when a quart or two of one of the early kinds may be sown for a late crop.

Laxton's Alpha will require sticks about thirty inches high; Champion of England, Telephone and Laxton's Prolific Long Pod will require sticks about four feet in height.

NOTE.—New varieties of Peas are coming forward from year to year and occasionally a variety appears superior, or fills a place not occupied by any other, and one who would keep up with the times in Pea growing, as in other departments of the garden, should be a careful reader of horticultural literature, and especially, know well what is offered new by enterprising seedsmen; not, in fact, to test all new varieties, but to accept those which have been proved to be good by sufficient trial.—EDITOR.

ONION CULTURE.

It is absolutely essential to success in Onion culture that the ground should be rich. Almost any soil that is free from sticks and stones, can be made to raise good Onions if it is thoroughly drained and fertilized; but the land that is right naturally is scarce.

My Onion patch is black ground, something like Illinois soil, naturally well drained, gravelly subsoil, and one side, perhaps one-third of the piece, quite gravelly. It is here that I raise my largest and best Onions. The piece contains three-fourths of an acre. It has had about forty loads of well-rotted manure each year for the last three years, it having been put on in the fall and plowed in, when possible to do so, immediately after the crop has been taken off. In addition to this, I have put about fifty bushels of unleached wood ashes on, each year, having spread it on the surface and harrowed it in just before seed sowing. I try to have the sowing done by the tenth of April at the latest.

The manner of preparing the ground is as follows: Plow as shallow as possible and cover the manure all up, say five or six inches. Harrow with an Acme harrow, as it draws the straw, etc., down into the ground; any harrow with the teeth slanting backwards is the best. After thoroughly harrowing, go over it with lump smasher or leveler, which is a plank concern, six feet square, put together like the clapboards of a house. It effectually pulverizes the surface, fills the horses' tracks, and leaves the ground level. Raking with a hand rake is expensive and it cannot be done so perfectly that the seeds, when sown with a Matthews' Drill, will not be unevenly covered. It may be necessary on some pieces to harrow and smooth several times. The ground must be very fine, and the firmer the better, if it is not actually hard. I can fit my Onion patch in this way in one day with a team. The variety I usually sow is the Yellow Globe Danvers.

The next thing is the cultivation. As soon as the Onions are large enough so that I can see the rows, I start the cultivator. I sow thirteen inches apart; the knife on the cultivator, which is a two wheeled one and works between or astride the rows, is eleven inches long, and this cuts within an inch of each row. I run the knife, which is two inches wide, just beneath the surface, and the ground is disturbed but very little; however, every weed which has sprouted is killed. Then I put on the little hoes, similar to those on Ruhlman's cultivator, set them an inch and a half apart, one on each side of the row, and go through them again. Then we get down on our hands and knees, or rather, elbows and knees, and weed them. I employ mostly men, as boys are usually not thorough enough. About three cultivatings and two weedings usually bring them through.

We pull them either with a wooden rake or with the hands; two men will pull a half acre in a day, if they are ripe. They should be allowed to lie three or four days in the sun after pulling, or until they are thoroughly dried; if placed in barrels or in piles before becoming thoroughly dry, they sweat and spoil very rapidly. The cheapest way is to top them in the field, and let them lie a day or two before putting into barrels or piles. This topping job is the most expensive part of it; it cost us about five cents a bushel to get the tops cut off, which should be done with a sharp knife, not with shears, as it detracts from the appearance of the Onions to have the top cut square off close down, and they are also more liable to rot.

The marketing of the crop was not included in the subject of this essay, or I would try to tell how we pack them, etc.

My first crop was about one hundred and fifty bushels on this same three-quarters of an acre; second crop nearly two hundred and fifty bushels; third, over three hundred, and this year we raised over four hundred bushels of merchantable Onions, besides about twenty bushels of the size HEINTZEL wants for pickles. The cause of the small ones was sowing a part of the patch too thickly. I find two and one-half pounds of good seed plenty for an acre, if it is all put in at an even depth, say from one-third to one-half an inch; if sown too thickly they will never get pulled out as they should be, and it injures those remaining to take part out.

The tools used in working the Onions should be so constructed as to draw the dirt from the plants rather than towards them, and in weeding it is well to be careful not to leave any more soil near them than enough to support them in an upright position. As much as possible of the weeding and cultivation should be done before they commence to form bulbs, yet if weeds are there it pays to take them out after they have commenced to bottom.

Onions will not bear neglect and make a profitable crop. Plenty of manure, thorough fitting of the ground, good seed, and clean cultivation are the essentials to success in the cultivation of Onions.

FIELD CULTURE OF ONIONS.

The demand the past few years for Onions has caused no little thought and experiment with wide-awake gardeners how to successfully meet it, and no doubt many, as I have done, have resorted to different methods of planting, cultivating, weeding, etc., and the best kind of tools have been practiced with to keep down the weeds and to improve the crop. In some places at the north the Onion can be raised on new ground by sowing broadcast, but not with good success, as the weeds most always get the advantage of them and choke them out. I never tried broadcasting but once.

My method is to select a rolling piece of ground, sloping to the south. The ground should be strong enough to raise a heavy crop of Corn; it should be plowed in the fall, so as to be ready to sow early in the spring, which is one of the most important points. As soon as the ground will work well, or in March or the first of April, harrow the ground thoroughly and run over the ground crosswise with a float made of two inch Oak boards, one foot wide and as long as desired; bolt three pieces together, lapping one on the other like clapboards, thus forming a most perfect clod-masher and leveler. Plant the seed in drills, not less than fourteen inches apart, and I prefer fifteen inches, and a half inch deep, using a reliable seed drill, and I can recommend the Matthews drill as the simplest and most perfect one in use.

As the seed is a long time in germinating, and weeds and grass are likely to get the start, the ground selected should be as free as possible from weed seed and kept clean. The Onion may be raised on the same ground several years with good results. After the tops appear an inch or so above the ground, start a careful man, not a boy, with the wheel hoe, passing twice in the row, shaving everything clean but the strip where the Onions stand. If the Ruhlman Wheel Hoe is used it will save the labor of at least six hands with the hand hoe. Many fail and give up at the hand weeding. This operation must be performed either with the fingers or with the small tools made for that purpose At this work boys, and girls, too, can be employed, and I would rather have one good girl than two boys, as the girls appear to realize the delicacy of the work, and set out at it more carefully. Every weed should be

FIELD CULTURE OF ONIONS.

pulled out, and the Onions thinned to two or three inches apart, and by doing this first weeding thoroughly the wheel hoe will nearly complete the cultivation, or at least till late in the season, so that one more hand weeding will be sufficient.

After the last weeding, keep the wheel hoe running, going over the patch every week, and the motion of the hoe will cut out and cover up nearly all the weeds. By the use of good seed, good ground, good tools to cultivate, and a little patience, a field of Onions can be raised with as much certainty and success as any other crop.

CULTIVATION OF ONIONS.

In order to obtain a successful as well as profitable crop of Onions, certain requisitions must be complied with. They are these: 1st, new, choice seed of the very best quality should be obtained; 2d, a suitable soil should be selected, and the most suitable manure obtained; 3d, the ground should be thoroughly prepared, and the seed properly sown, and last, but not least, the crop should be well cutivated and cared for.

LARGE RED WETHERSFIELD.

I know of no vegetable in which the quality of the seed has greater influence than the Onion, therefore, the greatest care should be taken to procure the very best, regardless of cost. Do not procure cheap Onion seed in any case, for most if not all of it is worthless, and will certainly prove to be very dear to the purchaser in the end.

The most suitable soil, and one that should be selected, if possible, is a very rich sandy loam, one that has been heavily manured and well cultivated for hoed crops for two or three years previously is the best, and I would impress this fact upon all, that it is entirely useless to attempt to raise Onions on a poor or unsuitable soil. Care should also be exercised in the proper selection of the

EARLY RED.

manure used for the crop. Nothing is better than good stable manure well decayed, and finely pulverized, and if a liberal quantity of bone-dust can be mixed with it, so much the better. Commercial or concentrated fertilizers are much esteemed by some,

CULTIVATION OF ONIONS.

and have been used with very satisfactory results, but it is well to be very careful in their use.

Suitable preparation of the soil is also of the greatest importance, and to accomplish it a considerable portion of the work should be done early in the autumn; all the refuse of previous crops should be collected and removed, and the manure applied at the rate of thirty to forty two-horse loads to the acre, spreading it as evenly as possible. The manure can then be plowed in to a moderate depth, or about five or six inches, and then a good dressing of bone-dust, wood ashes, or superphosphate of lime, may be given and worked in with a cultivator in the opposite direction to which it was plowed, and the ground left in this rough condition. Early in the spring, as soon as the ground is dry enough, cultivate again, then harrow it in all directions so as to thoroughly pulverize the soil and to have it as fine as possible.

YELLOW GLOBE DANVERS.

The seed should be sown very early in the spring, just as soon as the ground can be prepared. Sow in drills from sixteen to eighteen inches apart, being very careful to have the rows straight, in order to facilitate cultivation. Use a good seed drill for sowing, one with a roller attached for covering, and have it properly regulated for sowing the seed to the desired thickness, and cover it about half an inch in depth, remembering that thin seeding produces the largest Onions. From four to five pounds of seed will be sufficient to sow an acre. As soon as the Onions can be seen the length of the row, they should be hoed, just skimming the ground between the rows, using a scuffle or push hoe; in about two weeks hoe again. After this they should be thinned out and

WHITE GLOBE.

weeded, being careful not to disturb those that remain. In about two weeks they should be hoed and weeded again, and repeat the operation as often as necessary until the plants cease to grow.

As soon as the tops die down, the crop can be gathered, storing in a dry, cool, well ventilated room, spreading them out thinly at first, afterwards they can be placed more thickly, say four or five inches in depth. On the approach of cold weather close all windows and doors, and keep the temperature just above the freezing point, but if they happen to freeze it will not injure them unless they are permitted to thaw and freeze again. When Onions are raised in quantity a very popular method of keeping them is to spread straw on a barn floor to a depth of eighteen inches, on this spread the Onions, and cover with two feet or more of straw; in this way they will keep until May.

WHITE ITALIAN TRIPOLI.

Of the many varieties the following are the best for field cultivation and market purposes:

Large Red Wethersfield, of large size, very productive; the best keeper, one of the most popular for general cultivation.

Early Red, two weeks earlier than the above; of medium size, very productive.

Early Globe Danvers, of medium size, with a yellowish brown skin and white flesh and having a very mild flavor.

Large Yellow, or Yellow Dutch, is a very popular market variety, having a white flesh and mild flavor.

White Globe produces handsome globe-shaped bulbs of a very mild flavor.

White Portugal, a large, flat, mild-flavored Onion, not one o the best keepers.

For pickles, or set Onions, sow and treat as above advised, but do not thin them. Sow thickly, at the rate of forty pounds per acre; these little Onions, if planted in the spring, will form large Onions sooner than seed.

The Potato Onion produces a quantity of young bulbs around the parent root. They should be planted early in spring, in rows eighteen inches apart, six inches apart in the rows and one in depth; the large bulbs produce small ones, the small ones, large, alternately.

CULTIVATION OF ONIONS.

Top Set, or Button Onions, produce, instead of seed, a number of small Onions at the top of the stalk, which, if planted, will produce a large Onion much earlier than those from seed, the large Onion producing the top and the small top Onions the large ones. The little Onions are generally set out in the fall, in a manner similar to the Potato Onion, early enough to get a start before cold weather sets in.

The new Italian Onions, of which there are several admirable varieties, have a mild flavor, and grow to a very large size, often weighing from one to three pounds. They do best when grown in the garden, and are not profitable as a field crop. Top sets, Potato Onions, and Onion sets are recommended for an early small crop for home use, or a near market. Grown as a field crop they seldom, if ever, prove to be a profitable one.

RAISING ONIONS.

Having been engaged in the business of Onion culture some twelve years, I think I can, perhaps, give some points in that line, which will be of interest. Onions can be raised on almost any kind of soil. The best is a black, sandy loam; a fine, gravelly soil will produce good results; a light yellow loam will answer for an early crop; and a wet, clayey soil will do well for a late one. A liberal coating of manure should be given the land. Stable manure, with the straw well shaken out, is the best; and next to that, manure from the hog-pen. Rock-weed spread on in the fall, is very good, though when it is used I would recommend a top-dressing of guano. Dry sea-weed, cross-plowed in, in the fall, also answers a good purpose. I would recommend deep plowing at all times, never less than ten or twelve inches. Harrow well both ways, then rake with wooden hand-rakes, such as are used in haying, with the handles shortened, and the teeth shortened one and a half inches. The quantity of seed used should depend on the producing qualities of the soil. For a late crop on strong, healthy land, I should use six pounds per acre; on old land, well worn, eight pounds; for an early crop on new land, four to five pounds will be all that is necessary, and on old land six to eight pounds.

All seed should be sown soon as the ground is in fit condition— that is when the ground is dry or mealy, not wet, soggy, or frozen. The time will vary according to locality, from the first of April to the first of May. After planting, if the land is light and dry, roll with a hand-roller. I think the use of the roller enables one to begin hoeing sooner, as the plants can be seen almost as soon as they start. The machine I use for planting is a local one, which I have not yet seen in market. It plants two rows at a time, twelve inches apart, marks the third row, covers the seed and rolls the ground; it is pushed by hand. One man can plant one and a half acres a day. I commence hoeing as soon as the Onions begin to show in the row, and hoe at least three or four times during the season. I use the hoe in preference to weeding, as the latter tramples the ground so much, and wastes a great many Onions.

Of the many kinds of Onion seed sown, I consider the Red Globe best, both in regard to productiveness, and keeping qualities. Next to that comes the Yellow Danvers. I have planted three kinds of red Onion seed at the same date, and they matured as follows: Early Cracker Red, August 5th to 11th; Wethersfield Red, August 20th; Red Globe, August 30th to September 6th.

Potato Onions are easy to raise and bring a good return for the outlay.

Philadelphia sets also do well, though it is rather more work to plant them than Potato Onions, as they are smaller. Small red sets from Early Red Onions ripen about a week earlier than the first ones from seed.

One man can take care of about three acres of land, if he attends to his business. My brother and myself had seven acres of land on Long Island in 1861-2, which yielded three thousand, two hundred (3200) bushels of the best Onions I ever saw.

For a second crop on land where early Onions are planted, I would recommend Carrots. I have had great success in that line. I planted Carrots at second hoeing of Onions, on the 10th of May, on three-fourths of an acre of land, measured by surveying. On this piece of ground I raised six hundred bushels of Onions, and the same year, on the same land, I raised five hundred bushels of Carrots, and took a premium on the crop at our Queens County Fair.

Begin to harvest the Onions when the tops grow yellow and fall. I pull by hand, never using a rake, as they cure better by being carefully handled. Put three rows in one, with the bottom outward; let them remain in rows till the tops are thoroughly dried, or in a crackly condition, which will take from one to two weeks. If, however, they are wanted for shipment, top as soon as possible after pulling. Use a knife for topping, cutting about three inches from the Onion. The Onions must be thoroughly dried before housing for the winter. They keep well in bins made of slats, about five feet deep and four feet wide. Do not put more than one hundred and fifty to two hundred bushels in a bin, and put them all in the same day, as the addition of a second lot causes a second sweating, and induces decay. Keep as cool as possible, giving ventilation on every pleasant day, when it does not freeze outside. Freezing does not spoil them, however, if they are kept in that condition and not disturbed until spring. In conclusion, I would say that Onions, if strictly attended to, pay for the outlay better than Corn, Potatoes, or hay.

CABBAGE.

For growing the Cabbage to perfection a deep, rich, strong soil is necessary, especially for the later kinds, and the land ought, by all means, to be thoroughly drained. Good drainage, deep tillage and constant cultivation will ensure a heavy crop of Cabbage.

Presuming, then, that the land has been drained, it should be deeply plowed in the fall, so as to allow the frost to disintegrate its particles, sweeten it and render its inorganic properties fit for plant food; by this means it will also be suitable to work at least a week earlier in the spring, as the frost will leave it quicker, and the superfluous water drain from it sooner. The next thing is to get good seed from true stocks. Good Cabbage seed is easily known by being plump, round, and of a dull, rich, purplish brown color. Old seed gets a whitish gray, and to obviate this the seed is sometimes oiled and run through a mill, therefore, I would always be shy of shining, oily seeds; but no reliable seedsman will send out seed that will not grow at least seventy-five per cent., which is a pretty good average for Brassica oleracea. Above all, get it true, as on this depends the success of next year's harvest; avoid cheap samples. A good, true stock of any seed will always command a good price, as the seed-grower has to exercise a great deal of care and labor in cultivating, rearing, harvesting and cleaning; good seed is always cheapest, whatever price it is.

"TRUE" JERSEY EARLY WAKEFIELD.

For an early crop, Early Wakefield, Henderson's Summer and Winningstadt will be found good, reliable market sorts, and may be sown out of doors in the south-eastern States in the middle of September, but in the eastern, western and northern will require the protection of a cold-frame. But I very much prefer sowing in a hot-bed in January or February, giving all the air possible, and transplanting into other frames as the weather moderates, as by this means there is a more continuous growth, and healthier plants are obtained, which are less liable to run to seed. As soon as the ground is workable in spring a liberal dressing, and a barrowful over, of well rotted farm-yard manure should be spread on the ground intended for early Cabbage, and at once plowed in. I do not think the practice a good one, though much in vogue, of putting the manure on the land during the winter, for the melting snow and the spring rains wash much of its most valuable properties into the drains, and when the plant comes to want these very things, it finds them not, in fact, scarcely anything is left save the organic parts of what once was rich in minerals, salts and phosphates. Let the manure be carted straight from the heap and spread and plowed in at once, and the plant can draw from it all the season. After the plow, follow with a well weighted harrow, so as to thoroughly pulverize and mix the soil; do this thoroughly, as soil that is well worked in spring is much less liable to bake on the surface afterwards, and the sun and air permeate it to a much greater depth, and there is a more rapid and healthier growth, and as a natural sequence, earlier and finer Cabbage.

HENDERSON'S EARLY SUMMER.

The lines can be marked off two feet apart and the first dull or wet day the plants put out about eighteen inches apart, being about eight thousand to the acre, which ought to sell for from two to three hundred dollars. While the plants are growing, the cultivator should be run between the rows once every fourteen days, and the hoe between the plants as often as possible. Never let the weeds get more than an inch high, as a man can get over more ground then in one hour than he will in half a day a week or so later on. Early in June run the double share plow down the center of each row after the cultivator, and your early Cabbage will require very little more attention.

Late Cabbages are generally sown out of doors, in April and May, but I am not an advocate of this practice, as the Turnip flea is very plentiful, and although a good enough number of seedlings may be nursed up by the aid of smoke and soot, yet they very seldom escape scot free. "A much better plan is to sow in one of the frames that the early Cabbage were taken from, and cover with the sash or anything until such time as they attain their second leaf, when they may be dusted with soot, and the flea defied; but sow very thinly so as to get short, stocky plants, and if they come up too thick thin out and transplant, and half an hour spent this way will be well repaid in the future well-being of the plants.

The sorts I favor most are French Oxheart, Mammoth Marblehead, Excelsior Flat Dutch, Large Late Drumhead, Drumhead Savoy and Red Dutch.

As fall Spinach and early Potatoes will be cleared away in June or July, the land they have occupied may receive a heavy dressing of manure and be plowed deeply, and then be broken down with a good harrow, and furrows run two or three inches deep, and three feet apart across the plat; take advantage of the first favorable day for planting, and set your plants at least two feet apart in the bottom of the furrow; after this do not neglect the cultivator and hoe. The plants being in the bottom of the furrows get the advantage of the rainfall, which is only limited in July and August, and the hoe and cultivator gradually filling in the soil gives them a deeper roothold, and they are less liable to flag or get a check in growth in the hot, dry weather. Toward the middle of August they will be ready for earthing up, which can be done by the double share plow.

PERFECTION DRUMHEAD SAVOY.

As soon as the white butterfly, Pieris (Pontia) Brassicæ, begins to make love over the Cabbages, take the first dewy morning and sprinkle all the plants liberally with wood ashes; this will not only destroy the caterpillars but will also help the crop by supplying potash and bicarbonate of lime, and as often as the caterpillars are noticed at work take half an hour or so in the morning and go over the Cabbage plat with a box of wood ashes and give them a dose. In land deficient in lime the wireworm and white worm sometimes attack the roots, causing a collapse of the whole plant;

when this is noticed, lime water with a little flour of sulphur will exterminate them. Clubbing at the root very often proceeds from careless planting, doubling up the roots instead of making the hole large enough to admit of its going straight down, thereby causing a stoppage of sap, a consequent swelling or tumor which develops into what is called clubroot; therefore a little extra care in planting will very frequently obviate this evil altogether.

EXCELSIOR LARGE FLAT DUTCH.

The best mode I have found of storing Cabbage for winter and spring, is as follows: When it is deemed advisable to store the Cabbage, pull them up and turn their heads down for a day or so to drain all moisture from between the leaves, then remove all decayed and superfluous leaves, and put them three or five deep, roots inward, about one hundred in a pit or pile. Then cover with six or eight inches of soil, not less, for with a light covering they are too susceptible to atmospheric changes, and sudden thaws are very injurious to the well-being of the crop. When wanted for market a whole pit can be taken at once, hence my reason for recommending small pits; they keep better and are more manageable, for I have found when a pit is broken into and the air let in, the Cabbages never keep so well after.

NOTE.—The only reliable substance for the destruction of the Cabbage caterpillar, Pieris Brassicæ, is Pyrethrum powder, or the Insect Exterminator having Pyrethrum as one of its ingredients. The powder can be dusted on the plants quickly and cheaply by means of a bellows made for the purpose.—EDITOR.

CELERY.

I have always cultivated my own Celery, and what little I know about the matter has been learned by experimenting. I will try to tell, as simply as I can, what my experience has been.

For the past seven years I have, for the benefit of my health and love for out-door work, been my own gardener, and have taken charge of both vegetable and flower gardens. I have not only taken charge of them, but have done the work myself. Until the past six years the cultivation of Celery has not been carried on extensively here. It was thought to be a very tedious and difficult operation, and the majority of people considered it too much work, besides a great many did not know how to treat it. Six years ago, I made up my mind I would make the trial and see what I could do at Celery raising. It was then too late to get seed and raise my own plants. I happened to remember an old English gardener who raised plants of all kinds to sell, and accordingly I called upon him, and inquired if he had any Celery plants for sale, and what variety they were. He said he had plenty of the Boston Market, which he considered the best variety grown. I asked him if he thought I could raise Celery. "Why, certainly," says he, "if you can raise other vegetables you can raise Celery." He sold me some plants and gave me some information concerning the treatment they should receive. I went home with my plants and had a trench prepared after the following manner:

I had it dug about a foot deep; I then put in equal parts of wood ashes, dressing from the hen-house, and rich, black soil, which I worked up well together with a hoe. Then I set the plants about six inches apart, packing the dirt firmly at the roots, after which I gave them a good sprinkling twice a day until they had taken root enough to be firm in their places. Then I kept the trench nearly filled with water. I could do this very easily, for my garden bordered on a pond where I could dip the water up by the pail-full, and use it as freely as I wished. I had heard some one say Celery was a water plant, so I gave it plenty, and found that it agreed with it splendidly.

When the plants had made growth enough to cause the branches to lie over, I hilled them up a little, just enough to keep the stalks erect. I kept up the hilling process at intervals of about two weeks, all summer; always hilling when the weather was dry, and being careful to hold the stalks together with one hand to keep the soil from getting into the heart of the plants. As I wished to get some blanched early for our fair, which was to take place the fifteenth of September, I did the last hilling the first of September which gave it two weeks' time to bleach.

The heads were very large and branching, as I believe is usually the case with Boston Market. The stalks were white and crisp, and upon the whole was considered very nice Celery, and far exceeded my expectations. I exhibited some at our fair and was awarded first premium.

My second year's experience was as follows: Some of my friends suggested to me that Turner's Incomparable Dwarf was superior to Boston Market for the table. I concluded to get seeds of it and raise my own plants, and did so. Having no hot-bed, or any other proper convenience for raising the plants, I sowed the seeds in boxes and raised the plants in the house. Of course they did not have the same chance to grow that they would have had in a hot-bed, and had to be put out in the border when quite small. But they became good, stocky plants, and by the last of June were fit for trenching. I prepared the trench in the same manner as before, except, having no dressing from the hen-house, I used that from the blacksmith shop instead, which I think is far superior to the other, and the best fertilizer ever used among vegetables and plants, on account of having so much of the paring of the horses hoofs in it. I did not have water as handy as before, as we had removed to another place, and could not give the plants as much water as they needed, therefore did not get as large a growth, but the quality was good and the flavor was excellent. The flavor being better, I think, was owing to the variety. I exhibited some at the fair, in September, and was again awarded first premium, which made me think I was a captain at raising Celery.

My third year's experience. This year I concluded to raise two varieties. I bought, with other vegetable seeds, one package each of Turner's Dwarf and Sealey's Leviathan. Having sickness in my family I could do nothing about gardening until very late. The last of April I prepared a bed out of doors, on the south side of the house, in a sheltered situation, sowed the seed, and kept the bed moist by sprinkling it often. The seeds came up sooner than when I sowed them in the house. The plants made a rapid growth, and were very strong and thrifty. I prepared the trenches the same as before, and set the plants right from the seed bed, where they had made such a fine growth that it was not necessary to transplant them out in the border. In trenching, this year, I put the plants about five inches apart, and kept the trenches well filled with water, as I was living, this year, where I had a well in my garden. I used to pump the water into tubs, let it stand until warm, and then fill the trenches. The hilling process was about the same, hilling at intervals of about two weeks until the first of September, then I banked it clear to the top, and by the twentieth of September I had the most beautiful Celery you ever saw. The heads were large, the stalks two and a half feet long, very solid and crisp, and as white and smooth as polished ivory. I exhibited some at the fair, and was again awarded the first premium. Of the two varieties raised this year, I think Turner's is superior to the other; Sealey's Leviathan grew larger, but Turner's was crisper and of better flavor.

I think hilling at intervals all through the season to be an improvement for this reason: When the stalks are held together they shade each other, and almost the entire head will be crisp and fit for eating. Otherwise, if the stalks are allowed to sprawl about all summer, and hilled in the fall, there are many of the outside stalks that will be tough and never bleach enough to become fit for use.

My method of Celery culture is this: 1st. Send where you will get good seed.

2d. Prepare a seed bed out of doors in a sheltered situation. You will get your plants early enough by so doing, for they grow much faster and are much stronger than when grown in a hot-bed.

3d. Sprinkle the bed often to keep it moist, and when the young plants are about three inches high transplant them into rows, putting them three inches apart in the rows, and the rows about one foot apart.

4th. When the plants have become stocky, have a trench dug about one foot deep, put into it equal parts of wood-ashes and good rich dressing, and rich, black soil, and work altogether with a hoe.

5th. Set the plants about five inches apart, and be sure to straighten out the roots and press the soil firmly about them.

6th. Sprinkle them enough to keep them fresh until they are firm in their places, and then give them all the water you have a mind to, the more the better.

7th. When they have made growth enough to cause the branches to lie over, hill up enough to hold the stalks erect. Continue the hilling process at intervals of two weeks all summer, being careful to do it when the weather is dry, and in the afternoon when the dew is off. Be sure, when hilling, to hold the stalks together, to prevent the soil from getting into the heart of the plants.

8th. Such portion as you wish for early use bank to the top by the first of September; for winter use bank to the top from the first to the middle of October.

I think by following these instructions almost any one can raise Celery fit for a king, and when we get the varieties called White Plume and Chemin's introduced here, which need no banking, I think we can raise Celery fit for the queen.

KEEPING CELERY IN WINTER.

Hearing of so many failures in preserving Celery in winter, I am induced to give my experience in this matter. I used to put my Celery in trenches, as is more or less generally practiced; the result was, I had lost half of it, or more, by rotting, especially if there had been much rain during the fall and winter, after the vegetable had been stored away. After many annual losses, as well as suffering the inconvenience of Celery stored in trenches, where, often, in severe weather, it is either impossible to remove it with safety, or it is done with the greatest difficulty, I thought of a plan which has ever since proved successful in practice, and which I will now describe. I had a pit dug and prepared, which was completed in almost as short a time as it usually required to dig trenches.

The pit was made eight feet long, five feet wide and three feet deep. Two pieces of plank, each about ten feet long, were then placed along the sides of the pit at the ground line, and were let into the ground at each end, so that the upper edge of one was flush with the surface, while the other, on the opposite side, not being dropped so much, stood six inches above the surface of the ground. These planks formed the plates on which the roof rested, and one of them being higher than the other, gave the roof a pitch, and which was six inches for five feet, enough to carry off the rain falling on so small a surface. Three posts, one at each end and one in the middle, were placed under each plank, as supports. A roof was made of inch boards doubled so as to batten the cracks.

The entrance to the pit was gained by excavating a little in front of it and placing three or four steps in; the front of the pit was boarded and supplied with a door. A frame was placed around the dug-way entrance to the pit and covered with a rough door, placed on without fastening, so that it might easily be thrown entirely off. In the fall the roof is supplied with a covering of leaves four or five inches in thickness, which remains on all winter, preventing the hardest frost from entering the enclosure. In the spring the leaves are removed and both doors thrown open and the cave remains dry and airy during summer. This place was made several years since and still remains in good condition.

Before the Celery is put in in the fall, the ground at the bottom is forked three or four inches deep. When the Celery is dug, all the suckers and straggling leaves are removed, and then it is ready to be placed in winter quarters. I commence at the back side of the pit and, with a trowel, open a trench about three or four inches deep, and in this place the heads of Celery in an upright position, packing them closely together. The next trench is made so there will be a little space between the rows. In this manner the whole stock is placed away. A pit of the size here described will hold about three hundred heads of Celery.

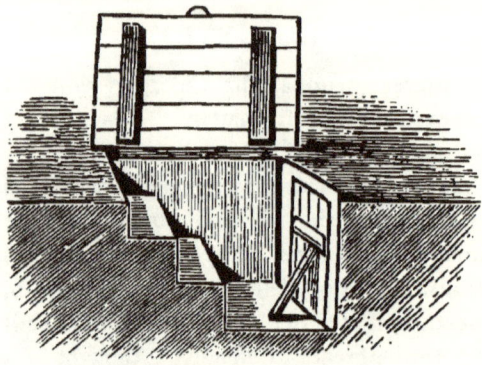

ENTRANCE TO CELERY PIT.

The advantage of this place is that you can open it every day and procure your daily supply fresh and sound, and not have the Celery lying around in the cellar for a week at a time until all its freshness and flavor are gone, as is generally the case where it is placed in the trenches, since a trench cannot be opened every day. I can go in the dark and take Celery out of my pit.

A pit of this style is never objectionable or offensive to the sight like a root-house, because it is made level with the surface of the ground and cannot be seen until one is close to it. It can be made in any corner, providing it is dry. Celery must be kept dry both above and at its roots; yet a cool, moist atmosphere is indispensable for keeping it crisp and good.

ROOT CROPS.

What root crops can be raised with profit for feeding cattle, and how?

Parsnips, Carrots, Turnips, both English and Swedish, and Beets can all be raised with more or less profit for feeding cattle. To do their best all require deep, rich, mellow soil. For Parsnips and Beets the ground should be well drained, either naturally or artificially. For Carrots, drainage is not so essential, excellent crops being often produced upon damp, undrained soils by late sowing, though always at some risk from superabundant moisture if the season be one of more than average rainfall. Turnips in variety being sown from June 1st to August 15th or later, when the weather is usually driest, and being least easily injured by wet of any of the root crops seem still more independant of drainage, though even they may have too much water. In all cases drainage benefits, not only by relieving the land of a superabundance, but by conserving a scanty supply of water.

We will now consider the different species of root crops in the order named above, which may, in a rough way, be also regarded as the order of desirability, beginning with the least profitable, although all have some special points to recommend them.

Parsnips should be sowed as early in spring as the earth will work reasonably dry and mellow. The ground should be plowed deeply, and if the subsoil is not of a friable texture it should be thoroughly loosened with a subsoil plow. On a small scale digging and trenching with the spade make excellent work, but wherever the size of the plat will permit, horse power is much the cheaper. When practicable, this preliminary preparation is best done during the previous fall, a liberal quantity of well-rotted manure being at the same time worked in. I consider the enriching and loosening the subsoil to the depth of eighteen to twenty-four inches, or more, quite essential to the best success, as the Parsnip roots will be found to taper more gradually, and, of course, be larger than if these operations be omitted. Some deep, gravelly loam soils, if sufficiently rich, may not require subsoiling, however, and it is upon them that Parsnip raising is most profitable. The ground being plowed, it is to be fined by harrowing, and leveled by planking, or, on a small scale, by raking.

Eighteen to twenty-four inches apart is the proper distance for the rows, and seed may be sown quite thickly, say at the rate of five or six pounds to the acre. Since scarcely any seed deteriorates by age more quickly than that of the Parsnip, it should be, like CÆSAR's wife, above suspicion. I have sowed two and even three-year-old seed, carefully kept, but in no case with as good results as fresh seed. Germination is not the sole test. It may take place under favorable circumstances, and yet the resulting plant be deficient in vitality. As soon as the rows can be traced by the appearance above ground of an occasional plant, a careful man with wheel or other hoe may be set to work to destroy weeds. I have found it a good plan not to go over the whole ground in this way, but simply to outline every row by hoeing a strip a few inches wide on each side of it, leaving the central strips to be done by horse power. A "Bean cultivator," set narrow, with slim shanks and nearly horizontal blades, which do not disturb the earth much, is a good implement to use with a careful horse and driver. I weed the rows by hand after this cultivation, and thin with hoe and fingers to five or six inches apart in the row when the plants are two to four inches high. Nothing is gained by crowding the plants in either direction. To have good roots they must have lusty tops. On a small scale, where all the work must be done by hand, intermediate rows of Lettuce, Radish, or other crop to be removed early, may be sowed, but in what may be called field work these are inadmissible. After-cultivation consists in removing weeds and keeping the surface mellow, both easily done, as the leaves soon cover the ground well.

Insect enemies are the Celery worm, Papilio asteria, which are not very numerous and for which hand picking is the remedy, and another larva whose name I have been unable to learn, which feeds upon the young seed of the Parsnip, spinning a web for protection. It seldom attacks Parsnips the first year unless neglected seed-bearing plants stand near. Paris green, or pyrethrum, applied to these would probably be effectual to prevent its invading the former. It never troubled me but once, and then to a slight extent only.

In harvesting all root crops, the best plan is to cut off the tops before digging. The left hand gathers and grasps the leaves while the right hand, armed with a sharp knife, cuts them close to the crown, when they should be thrown in piles. Lively boys make rapid work of it. While upon the subject, I may add that the

ROOT CROPS.

knife had better be dispensed with in topping Beets, a smart twist being sufficient for each one. As Parsnip roots grow wholly under ground, and good ones are eighteen inches to twenty-four long, harvesting them is not easy. The best way is to run a deep furrow close by the row, follow with the subsoil plow, if one has it, and do the rest with spade and hands, one man digging and another pulling. Parsnips dry rapidly when exposed to the air. If harvested in the fall they should be stored in sand for culinary use; but for cattle they may be kept in pits in the open ground, or in an ordinary root cellar, not too dry, but care must be taken in all cases to prevent heating. Parsnips are often left in the ground all winter, being greatly improved in saccharine quality by frost. I have found Hollow Crown an excellent variety, but there are others equally good. Horses, cattle, sheep aud hogs are alike fond or Parsnips. For muscle, fat, milk, wool, and good condition generally, they are unsurpassed by any other root. The yield ranges from one hundred bushels of scraggy roots to six or eight hundred of fine, large, smooth ones, and the cost may range from thirty cents a bushel for the poor roots, down to ten cents, or less for the best. Choose ye!

Carrot seed, being rather slow of germination, I have had the best success by soaking it in scalding water. In fact, I pour upon it sufficient boiling water to float imperfect seeds and other trash, which I immediately skim off and throw away. The water is then immediately drained from the perfect seed, which is dried for sowing by mixing with it loam or plaster. No danger need be apprehended of spoiling good seed in this way. If the ground is properly moist the young plants will make their appearance as soon as the weeds do, if not before, instead of being smothered at birth as they often are. Carrot seed should not be sowed in dry earth, except, possibly, when rain is imminent, and then it were better to wait until the rain be over. The same remark applies to other seeds pretty generally. Four pounds of seed as sold, if good, is ample for an acre.

The preparation of the ground for Carrots should be as thorough as for Parsnips. Rent of land and cost of cultivation being the same, the profit in raising roots results in a judicious expenditure of manure and labor before the seed is sowed. But all gross, unfermented manures are objectionable unless applied to the soil a sufficient length of time in advance to become decomposed. In this connection it may be added that superphosphate of lime is an excellent dressing for land intended for roots. Two hundred to six hundred pounds may be applied by sowing broadcast and harrowing in.

The time of sowing Carrots, distance apart for the rows, distance in the rows and general cultivation are the same as for Parsnips. Carrots, however, are more impatient of neglect in the early stage than any other root crop. Until thoroughly established, weeds must not at any time be allowed to crowd them. Neither do the leaves cover the ground as well as those of Parsnips, and therefore weeds have a better chance to start throughout the season. A little attention to the removal of tall weeds well repays the careful cultivator. In thinning Parsnips and Carrots care must be taken to leave no two plants closer together than two inches, as in such a case the roots are apt to wind around each other and both be spoiled. The Celery worm is the only enemy of the Carrot here, and it is never very troublesome.

Harvesting, which should be done before very severe frosts in the fall, is conducted as for Parsnips. The remarks made under the head of storing Parsnips apply to all root crops, and need not be repeated.

The Belgian Carrots, white and orange, and the Altringham, all of which grow partly above ground, are extensively raised for stock-feeding; but although they have the decided advantage of being more easily harvested, and the doubtful one of producing a greater bulk, I prefer some of the shorter-growing, finer-fleshed varieties. Yields of a thousand bushels, and even more, are reported, but five hundred or six hundred bushels is probably the average.

But, be it remembered by the reader, there is no use trying to raise Carrots with profit unless you have time and inclination to attend to them in season.

One advantage the Turnip has over the roots already treated, is that the best time for sowing it is six to ten or twelve weeks later. Not only is the time from its seeding to its harvest shorter, but since much of its growth takes place late in the fall, when weeds are not so numerous nor so rampant, the labor of cultivation is, on the whole, much less.

Between June 15th and July 4th, when a soaking rain having fallen the previous night, the earth is too wet for cultivating Corn, and the weather is yet too unsettled to touch the hay, the farmer may turn to the piece of ground which was manured, plowed,

ROOT CROPS.

harrowed and set aside six weeks ago for Ruta Bagas. If not already rich enough, a dressing of well rotted manure should be spread upon the surface, the ground be then plowed again, harrowed and rolled or planked until thoroughly fine. The "planker" was originally a stone-boat, with smooth bottom, three feet wide by six feet long, but it is now improved by fastening the planks crosswise, lapping like clapboards on a house. Its width has also been extended until it is of square form.

I have struck out the rows for Swedes on the level surface, but prefer ridges. The ridges cost some labor to make, and are, theoretically, at least, drier than the level ground. On the other hand, upon them a beating rain is not so apt to wash the earth over the young plants, and the Bean cultivator, or even the ordinary Corn cultivator, carefully handled, may be run between the rows while the plants are yet small, without outlining the rows previously, as recommended in cultivating Parsnips. I form the rows with the shovel plow, making them twenty-four to twenty-eight inches apart, the latter by preference. The top is smoothed with a garden rake and the seed drilled in at the rate of two pounds per acre.

The advantage of pressing the earth into close contact with the seed cannot be too highly insisted upon.

As soon as up, dust the Ruta Baga plants with air-slacked lime, plaster, soot, ashes, superphosphate, or road dust, to repel the flea. Later, the Cabbage plant-louse, Aphis brassicæ, is sometimes troublesome. As it works principally on the lower side of the leaf it is pretty hard to get at it with any application. The best remedy is to keep the plants growing rapidly by thorough cultivation. The Cabbage worm, Pieris rapæ, is another enemy, but owing to the spreading leaves of the Turnip it does but little damage. Still another enemy is the Radish maggot, which works in the root. It is much less troublesome upon new or fresh ground than upon old garden soil.

When three or four inches high and past danger from the flea, thin the plants to ten or twelve inches apart in the row. It is not profitable to raise Ruta Bagas on land upon which they must be left closer than nine or ten inches, at least. No set rule can be given as to the number of times to hoe or weed any root crop. The surface must be kept mellow and free from weeds; that is all.

The yield of Ruta Bagas runs from four hundred to one thousand bushels per acre. All farm animals are fond of, or can be taught to like Ruta Bagas. The only objection to them is that they impart a peculiar taste to milk and butter, but this can be easily avoided by feeding the cows immediately after milking.

White or English Turnips may be sowed from July 15th to September 1st. The value of the White Turnip is principally as a catch-crop on land otherwise good, but too wet for an earlier crop; also, on land from which an early crop of Potatoes, Peas, etc., has been removed. In either case it is well to plow the ground, harrow, roll, and harrow again a week or two before sowing, leaving it somewhat rough until a good shower of rain falls, after which it should be stirred with a cultivator and fined as thoroughly as may be. If the seed be drilled in, the rows may be twenty to twenty-four inches apart, the plants to stand, after thinning, six to ten inches apart. Two pounds of seed may be sown to the acre; less might answer, but it is well to err on the safe side. White Turnips are often sowed broadcast, but this is not usually the best way, as cultivation must be done altogether by hoe and fingers. Yet, under exceptionally favorable circumstances, upon new land, free of weeds, with very thin but even seeding, extraordinarily large crops have been thus raised at a minimum of cost.

Crop ranges from two hundred to twelve hundred bushels per acre.

The land for Mangels is to be prepared precisely as for Ruta Bagas, except that the ridges and rows may be twenty-four to thirty inches apart; I make them twenty-eight. What has been written above as to the cultivation of Ruta Bagas applies to this crop as well, except that the distance apart of the plants in the row should average about thirteen inches.

Success in all root crops depends, in some measure, upon proper thinning. The temptation is to leave too close a stand. It seems a pity to sacrifice a fine, thrifty plant!

If I have written enthusiastically of all the roots, it is because I think each good in its place. The profit in raising them is not that one may produce them at an expense of ten cents per bushel and sell them in market for twenty, but that they may be disposed of in the home market to the animals of the farm. They will pay for them in bright eyes, smooth coats, healthy lungs and bowels, and all that these imply.

www.ingramcontent.com/pod-product-compliance
Lightning Source LLC
Chambersburg PA
CBHW022145160426
43197CB00009B/1440